ETHAN NICHTERN

The Dharma of *The Princess Bride*

Ethan Nichtern is a senior teacher in the Shambhala Buddhist tradition and a teacher-in-residence for the Shambhala NYC community. He is the author of *The Road Home: A Contemporary Exploration of the Buddhist Path* and *One City: A Declaration of Interdependence*. In 2007, he founded the Interdependence Project, a nonprofit organization dedicated to secular Buddhist study as it applies to transformational activism, mindful arts, and Western psychology. Nichtern has taught meditation and Buddhist studies courses and retreats across the "Kale Belt" since 2002. He lives in New York City with his wife and baby daughter.

ALSO BY ETHAN NICHTERN

*The Road Home: A Contemporary
Exploration of the Buddhist Path*

*One City: A Declaration
of Interdependence*

The Dharma of *The Princess Bride*

THE DHARMA OF
THE PRINCESS BRIDE

What the Coolest Fairy Tale of

Our Time Can Teach Us About

Buddhism and Relationships

ETHAN NICHTERN

NORTH POINT PRESS

A division of Farrar, Straus and Giroux | New York

North Point Press
A division of Farrar, Straus and Giroux
175 Varick Street, New York 10014

Copyright © 2017 by Ethan Nichtern
All rights reserved

Published in 2017 by North Point Press
First paperback edition, 2018

The Library of Congress has cataloged the hardcover edition as follows:
Names: Nichtern, Ethan, author.
Title: The dharma of The princess bride : what the coolest fairy tale
  of our time can teach us about Buddhism and relationships /
  Ethan Nichtern.
Description: First edition. | New York : North Point Press, 2017. |
  Includes bibliographical references.
Identifiers: LCCN 2016059269 | ISBN 9780865477766 (hardcover) |
  ISBN 9780865478381 (e-book)
Subjects: LCSH: Princess bride (Motion picture) | Buddhism in
  motion pictures.
Classification: LCC PN1997.P74534 N53 2017 | DDC 791.43/72—dc23
LC record available at https://lccn.loc.gov/2016059269

Paperback ISBN: 978-0-86547-777-3

Designed by Richard Oriolo

Our books may be purchased in bulk for promotional, educational, or
business use. Please contact your local bookseller or the Macmillan
Corporate and Premium Sales Department at 1-800-221-7945, extension
5442, or by e-mail at MacmillanSpecialMarkets@macmillan.com.

www.fsgbooks.com
www.twitter.com/fsgbooks • www.facebook.com/fsgbooks

This book has not been authorized, licensed, or prepared by
any person or entity involved in the creation or production
of either the film or the book version of *The Princess Bride*.

For Grandpa Sol and "Grandpa" Chogyam:
As you wish.

For the Real Buttercup: As you wish.

For our Child, just arrived: Let's tell some stories.

CONTENTS

The Dharma of *The Princess Bride*

Introduction

Fairy Tales, the Real World,
and True Love

HELLO. MY NAME IS ETHAN NICHTERN. THE SIX-
Fingered Man was my father's best friend. Prepare to read.

David Nichtern and Christopher Guest were born two
weeks apart and grew up together in downtown New York
City. Christopher was not yet a diabolical villain with an
extraneous digit, nor one of the greatest comedic actors of
his time. David was not yet a Buddhist, much less a Buddhist

teacher. What they shared was an urban childhood and a love of making music (bluegrass, mostly, more or less the hip-hop of kids from the Village in the early 1960s). In their friendship, Chris was never the sadistic Count Rugen. Instead, he played a part more like Andre the Giant's Fezzik, defending my father against playground bullies. I have heard many stories of their swashbuckling together like Inigo Montoya and the Dread Pirate Roberts, unsheathing guitars instead of swords. They moved through city adventures from west to east, from Waverly Place to Stuyvesant Town—having fun, storming castles, being kids.

Christopher's role in *The Princess Bride* was the reason I was excited to see the movie when it was first released in the fall of 1987. I was nine years old. All I knew was that this man I had known all my life played a bad guy (a hilarious idea in itself) and that the movie was a kind of fairy tale, but not just any fairy tale. Even upon first viewing it, I knew the film was a parody. It felt like a sarcastic Xerox of the fairy-tale genre, as if a smart older kid were making fun of some cheesy story I'd already seen a thousand times.

I remember enjoying the movie that first time; it displaced my troubled mind into humor and fantasy during a particularly rough stretch of childhood, a yearlong span that included my parents' difficult divorce, my grandparents' double suicide, and, like a candle torched at both ends, the premature death of my parents' Buddhist teacher, the man who exerted a central gravitational pull in the galaxy of their lives (and later mine), the brilliant and enigmatic Chögyam Trungpa Rinpoche.

On top of all that trauma, there was the day-to-day

chaos of fourth grade. My best friend had skipped forward a grade without me after third grade, leaving me to fend for myself. Fending for myself was a difficult task, because I had two surgeries that year to help with a mild case of cerebral palsy on my right side. Surgery left me outcast, in a cast, for a significant portion of the school year. My best friend skipping ahead and my gimp status together made me, objectively speaking, the second least popular kid in my class. Sadly, this popularity ranking happened at a hippy New York City school founded in the 1960s on Dr. Martin Luther King Jr.'s vision of an inclusive multicultural society. This wonderful school preached nothing but diversity and acceptance daily—a sign that even the best utopias hold popularity contests. Fortunately for me, I still had one friend at school that year. Unfortunately for both of us, his social spasms, angry demeanor, and prepubescent unibrow made him, also objectively speaking, the number one least popular kid in our class.

Our friendship was mostly circumstantial and far from ideal. But still, he was my friend, my only real friend that year—that is, until, like the worst Buddhist kid in the world, I told him we couldn't hang out anymore, that he was dragging me down. His gruff demeanor crumbled as he started to cry. It was an awful move on my part, a classic case of the weak abandoning the weaker. Thirty years later, my choice still haunts me occasionally during sessions of compassion meditation.

Going to see *The Princess Bride* that first time was a great escape. In it were swashbuckling friends, ridiculous villains, and a valiant quest for the love of a lady with a very strange name. Most important, there was a grand-father using this wacky tale to comfort his grandson (almost exactly my age) on a sick day from school. Because I wanted to stay in bed and play Nintendo for most of fourth grade, I could easily relate. Much of the movie's existential brilliance was lost on me, though. I was just looking to escape: escape my parents' fighting, escape the indecipherable popularity contest at school, escape the truth of my suffering, and maybe escape this version of Earth altogether. I liked the movie's goofy action. It was a story with just a few, but not too many, "kissing parts."

Only much later, after many more viewings, did I learn that *The Princess Bride* was beloved by so many. When I say "beloved by so many," I am talking about a pirate ship that slowly sailed far beyond cult status, anchoring itself now in the very heart of the American postmodern canon. Just ask your friends: an abnormally large percentage of humans between the ages of two and two hundred now revere, or at the very least respect, this movie. (The few people I've met who haven't seen it often express knowing embarrassment at their cinematic omission.) At its mere mention, many people will pause and enter a visualization, an inner kingdom of bright nostalgia and appreciation. As far as anyone can tell, the film's retroactive popularity was unforeseen. When the movie was released, the novel by William Goldman on which his faithfully adapted screen-play was based was not well known, at least not among us Gen Xers. The film grossed only $31 million in theaters that year, making it the forty-first most popular film at the box office in 1987.[1]

As I grew older, I kept returning to the movie again and again, across three decades of growing up, a process of maturation that now (in my late thirties, even after decades of studying and teaching Buddhism) may still just be getting under way. Many other people I know went through a similar process with *The Princess Bride*. As the movie aged, and as those of us who were the Grandson's (Fred Savage's) age grew up (or *tried* to), it caught on, and became enshrined as an irrefutable staple of Generation X culture. The mixology-obsessed cocktail bar down the block from my Brooklyn apartment serves a mezcal-based drink (though brandy would be more appropriate) called the Inigo Montoya. The glass even comes with a toothpick sword across the rim, exacting heroic revenge against a six-sectioned slice of orange. The bar is one of many establishments I've been to that reference the movie on their menus. In 2015 the statistical website FiveThirtyEight conducted a survey of the twenty-five most rewatchable movies of all time—ever. *The Princess Bride* was number six. Among a particularly large swath of the population, a population that shares a wounded optimism about our society's ability to experience true love, and a rapier-quick sense of irony, the movie is surely number one. It is full of so many popular one-liners that whenever it is mentioned, people trip over themselves to choose which line to quote, hoping the person they are talking to doesn't know the story quite as well as they do. More often than not, they are wrong.

The Princess Bride is a story that's funny, sad, and poignant, a tale in which, after many sarcastic turns, true love wins the day. Twice. I sometimes quote the movie in my

lectures on Buddhism. When discussing the human tendency to idealize and objectify romantic love, I'll say something like "Whether you're looking for Prince Charming
or Princess Buttercup . . ." Generally, it turns out, more
people in the audience get the reference to Princess Buttercup than to Prince Charming.

I estimate that I've seen *The Princess Bride* on average
once per year since 1987—maybe thirty screenings. My
estimate is quite conservative, so you don't think I'm weird.
While a few amnesiac years passed without any viewings,
a few single days that were stormy both inside and out
included multiple rewinds (or, later on, multiple clicks).
I have watched it alone and with friends. I've watched it
while single, and I've watched it on dates. I've watched it as
a litmus test for compatibility with lovers, and I've watched
it while grieving those who turned out not to be my Princess Buttercup. I've watched it while bored, and I've watched
it while lamenting nothing but the grinding passage of
time. I've watched it while missing my grandparents and
fighting with my parents. And I've watched it when I didn't
want to meditate. In a not-too-distant future, I hope to watch
it with my children and, perhaps, if they wish, *as they wish*,
my grandchildren.

I am not going to say that the story of *The Princess
Bride* taught me how to love—that would be ridiculous. Living a human life, one dotted with confusion and composed
of intermittent periods of mindfulness and compassion,
has taught me what I know about love. The purpose of this
book is to pay respect to the cultural companionship we
each must keep while trying to deepen our spiritual lives.

It's an homage to the stories that keep us feeling safe as we navigate the uncomfortable path of self-discovery.

All of us, I believe, have held on to pieces of pop culture as we've proceeded on our own spiritual journeys. My most consistent companion has been *The Princess Bride*. As for the movie's relation to Buddhism—it may be correlation rather than causation, but here's the truth: almost everything I know about relationships, I learned over the past thirty years of doing two things that seem to have very little to do with each other—loving *The Princess Bride* and practicing Buddhism.

No Such Thing as a Relationship Expert

THE OTHER THING YOU NEED to know about me, besides my loving a postmodern fairy tale, is this: I teach Buddhism, or "Awake-ism," to use my own, more literal and accessible translation of the Sanskrit term. Another Sanskrit word, *dharma*, refers to any gathered body of teachings. This book is therefore the gathered teachings and experiences that have been useful to me while studying relationships and loving this movie. While the traditional teachings of Awake-ism focus on mindfulness in a personal and intimate manner, students of Buddhism find that the vast majority of what we deal with along the path of awakening has to do with our relationships. (Sometimes I think that if we didn't have to deal with relationships, we would probably be enlightened already.) If you ask people why they are really interested in studying Buddhism, and you dig (not very) deeply, you will almost always find your way to a conversation about difficulties they have understanding themselves in relationship to other people and to the world. From this struggle arises the search for a "master," the expert, or "guru," whose blessings we wish to receive. We long to find a genuine hero of living well in relationships, an emotional healer like Miracle Max, or else a Man (or Lady) in Black who has mastered love, someone who can let the rest of us in on the secret before we commit any more of the classic blunders.

I have worked with thousands of people on the practice of meditation, and it turns out, after all, that nobody comes to meditation looking to find their breath. Nobody is looking for a mantra. Nobody is looking for a teacher, or an altar, or a shrine, or even a community to practice with—although all these things often prove helpful to what we are seeking. What folks always come looking for is a way to be more present, less stressed, and more effective in life. Occasionally a student wants to leave her whole life behind and immerse herself in a long, solitary retreat. But what is a retreat, anyway? A retreat just means you crave some time and space away from your claustrophobic human relationships.

So, it really is this simple: we get on the spiritual path because either we want tools for our relationships or we want to escape those relationships for a while. We want to escape relationships only because we think we lack the tools to deal with other people sanely. Regardless, relationships, and our struggles with them, are the crux of any spiritual path.

In one word, life is about *interdependence*. Life is a web

of relationships, a cohort of people rubbing up against, and rubbing off on, one another. We each fumble through life for a brief series of moments, anchored only by our connection with our own minds, and our connection with other beings. Sometimes the web of human relationships around us feels grounding and supportive. Sometimes it feels like a sticky trap, a spiderweb.

Modern neuroscience demonstrates how social we human beings are. You only really know you are alive because you relate your own feelings and calibrate your own nervous system with those of other people: people called family, people called friends, people called colleagues. Then there's the gargantuan question of romance—how to use tools like Tinder mindfully and Match.com compassionately, how to survive the inevitable heartbreaks. Maybe (if it's your thing) you're wondering how to find your Prince Charming or your Princess Buttercup, or how to stay present with your match after you've already found them, or after you've started raising new little princes and princesses together. What would life be without all these relationships? It wouldn't be much at all—nothing that any human could recognize at least.

The "dharma" contained in *The Princess Bride* is all about relationships. The story offers a perfect canvas upon which to explore the three things that almost always take over the discussion when I teach Buddhism: the dharma of friendship, the dharma of romance, and the dharma of family. First, you have one of the best on-screen friendships ever: the circumstances that bring together the Spaniard Inigo Montoya, the giant Fezzik, and later Westley (aka

Farmboy, aka the Man in Black, aka the Dread Pirate Roberts) on a quest for vengeance and love. Second, you have a tale of romance with more insight than any rom-com I've ever seen or been forced to sit through. Buttercup and Westley reunite and discover how their love can be realized despite the obstructing forces of a hilariously greedy, delusional, and war-mongering world. Third, and most important, you have the tender truth of family: the Grandfather and Grandson privately sharing this fairy tale in the "real" world, on a sick day in suburban Chicago.

You might seek guidance in other relationships, such as those in your career, creative practice, or social justice work. But if you become more mindful in your personal relationships, then the relationships with coworkers or creative partners, or any other members of society you can think of, will only flourish. After all, as many masters have noted, the hardest relationships to imbue with spiritual principles are usually the most intimate ones. Chögyam Trungpa Rinpoche, the modern founder of the Shambhala Buddhist tradition I study and teach, once said, "It's possible that you could become enlightened everywhere *except* around your family." In the Zen tradition, there is a saying: "If you want to know if a master is truly enlightened, ask their spouse." We don't have to get "enlightened" to benefit from our intimate relationships, but the message is clear: if you learn about mindfulness or empathy by working with those closest to you, then your relationship with everyone else will be illuminated. That is, if you can figure out family, romance, and friendship, you can handle just about anyone or anything. If you work on your own relationships

wholeheartedly, that might grant you the insight necessary to change the world. Maybe you could even deal with
a mean old politician—say, Texas senator Ted Cruz, who is,
surprisingly, one of this movie's biggest fans. (A former
presidential candidate, Cruz does magnificent impressions
of multiple characters in this movie, especially Billy Crystal's Miracle Max. This fact might complicate our moral
understanding of *The Princess Bride*. Of course, after Miracle Max's heart is touched by love, he comes to believe in
accessible health care for the poor. Ted Cruz . . . not so
much. Cruz's confusion about the political meaning of the
movie led to Inigo Montoya himself, Mandy Patinkin, taking Cruz to task in a *Time* magazine op-ed.)[2]

I hold the title of a senior Buddhist teacher in a lineage
with deep roots in Tibetan spiritual and psychological
wisdom, and I've held this title since the age of thirty-two.
People, therefore, look to me as an expert on life, requesting
all kinds of advice on situations with which I sometimes
have very little personal experience. It's fascinating how
often people want to be told what to do in relationships. We
all want someone who knows what they are talking about
to be our guide through the Fire Swamps of fear, pain, desire, and miscommunication. And there's a lot of theoretical advice out there, opinions that suggest we treat human
relationships as some kind of "game" to win, or some kind
of karmic sweepstakes for which we only need to scratch off
a lottery ticket or learn a few "secret" tricks of the trade.

From a Buddhist standpoint, there's nothing to win in a
relationship, just as there's nothing to win in life—except, of
course, the deep satisfaction that comes from appreciation,

collaboration, and love. When all that fortune cookie wisdom and quasi-spiritual advice about how to "get what you want" fails, when we find ourselves struggling to communicate clearly or to connect fully with others, we get depressed and think, "I guess I'm just bad at relationships." I've recognized some version of this thought crawling around in the not-so-friendly nooks of my own mind so many times that I've lost count.

Guess what: everyone is bad at relationships, at least when it comes to making mistakes. In my humble opinion, nobody is "great" at this dance of desire, love, and humanity. While I might be considered a relative authority on meditation or Buddhist psychology, I am definitely no master of relationships. And I don't think anyone else is, either.

That's right, *nobody* is a relationship expert. Let me be clear: Of course, certain professionals have extensive psychological training to help others with their relationships. I am not claiming that this training is in any way invalid. Seeking relationship guidance from a third party with the skills to help can be one of the smartest and most humbling things we ever do. But the only way to progress with relationships is to connect with our longing to know ourselves more deeply, and to extend that longing to knowing others as well. By definition, no single person can be an expert at relationships. Every relationship is a collaboration between (at least) two people, and an expert is one lone person. A relationship is a movement beyond oneself, a stretch outside the private domain of experience. The very act of relating to another human being is the act of relinquishing your expertise. So "relationship expert" is an oxymoron, and no one should pretend to be anything that has the word *moron* in it.

Buddhism, however, does offer tried-and-true wisdom on how to work with all the tricky, awkward, and painful states of mind that arise in relationships. It teaches us how prepare for the obstacles we face, especially those tough moments in which we are triggered by the difficulties of human interaction—all the pain, fear, and miscommunication we encounter. One of the most powerful aspects of Buddhist teaching, especially the teachings on compassion, is its ability to allow us to recognize when we are caught by habitual patterns. This recurrent triggering[3] happens in an intensified way within the intimate relationships involved in close friendship, romance, and family life.

Even if your dharma practice is consistent and wholehearted, it won't stop you from being triggered by desire or disappointment, or any other feeling on the vast palette of human emotions. Practice does not stop you from feeling, ever. If you are looking to stop feeling, good luck with that. From the standpoint of the Shambhala tradition, the whole problem we face is that we've learned all too well to grow numb to our feelings. This avoidance leads to a limited, cocooned experience of life, trapping us in a mostly dead state. All the practices that I know will probably lead you to feeling *more*. Mindfulness brings you slowly back to life from your distracted, cynical, stressed-out way of being. What contemplative practices can provide is the mental space to see the present moment in the context of awareness and love and, over time, to choose different reactions when you are triggered by karma, your habitual patterns and defense mechanisms.

Life is the opposite of theoretical, which is what makes it miraculous. After all the advice you might get about dating, you just have to show up to the date. After all the therapy you might receive to deal with your parents or your children, the therapist can't live with these people for you. Nowadays, many of my friends are parents of young children. There are so many theories on parenting, so many of them published and popular and scattered on the bookshelves in the homes of people I love. These books contain complex theories, running the spectrum from attachment parenting to nonattachment parenting. But everyone I know who is a parent, after reading hundreds of books containing a few very helpful tips, says some version of what a close friend recently said: "Being a parent is so *intuitive*! It's the most ungeneralizable experience of my whole life. The only way to do it is to *do it*!"

Intuitive could be a synonym for the new cultural catchword *mindful*. Mindfulness involves a set of defined meditation practices, yes. But more than that, mindfulness is a frame of reference for one's life, a proclamation that the present moment is paramount. Our repeated return to *now* when we wander is the key to harmony and fulfillment in this or any other world. Mindfulness is about showing up and learning from that master known as direct experience. The only way to learn is to learn how to pay attention, and the only way to learn about relationships is to consciously make them our path. This requires the willingness to have no freaking clue what we are doing and to make tons of mistakes, often painful ones, with lessons absorbed over years, decades, and lifetimes. Sometimes Buddhism is referred to as a path of not knowing (also called "beginner's mind"), but I like to think of it as the path of being willing to have no clue and still be curious. Here's the most important question you could ask a teacher: "Tell me, oh master, how do I properly live life without having a clue how to relate to these people in front of me?" In the beginning, middle, and end, there is only one real answer to this question: "Just show up. And practice. A lot."

The Best Spiritual Teachings Come from Personal Experience, Not Ancient Lists

SOME OF MY FAVORITE TEACHERS are philosophical masters. Deft, witty, and inconceivably ambidextrous with their material, they are the Dread Pirate Roberts of their given subject. Regardless of the field of study, it's always awesome when the teacher knows history, context, and technique backward and forward. As a student, you always feel safer in the hands of a teacher who knows how to frame the topic. Yet no matter how smart a teacher may be, theoretical knowledge is not what we live for as students. What we live for, what we would cross oceans and scale cliffs to hear, are the personal stories of our teachers. Something amazing happens when a teacher leaves abstract philosophy or psychology behind for a moment and gets personal. Students lean in. They feel inspired by the sudden force of real humanity. It's like a cool breeze of relatability flowing into a room stagnated by the stale air of concepts.

When my main teacher, Sakyong Mipham, takes a break from leading esoteric practices during an intensive Tantric meditation retreat and starts telling a story about a recent bedtime conversation with his wife or daughters, or when he shares a childhood memory of his late father, Chögyam Trungpa, a story that no one has heard before, a hush comes over the room. Suddenly, everyone feels like family, even when hundreds of people are present.

When the most famous author in my tradition, Pema Chödrön, starts discussing the anger and disappointment she felt upon discovering that her husband was cheating on her—she threw rocks at him—I feel much closer to her than when she is talking about abstract notions of suffering and emptiness. I want to *know* this woman. I want to know the woman who threw that rock at her husband and later became a Buddhist Jedi! Whenever I open up to my own students about my experiences, my mistakes, my clueless moments, that's when true connection starts.

Some Western theorists have argued that total nondisclosure, a complete refusal to discuss one's own human process, is the best way for any healer to help. In this way, patients/students have no escape from themselves, no chance to deflect from working with their own personal experiences. I see the purpose of not distracting students from a focus on their own minds, but I mostly disagree with this stance of nondisclosure, a defensive stance against the human "master's" humanity being accidentally unmasked, their human awkwardness exposed. Sometimes, if you try too hard to be a mirror for someone else, you end up coming across like a brick wall. What we students thirst for, I believe, are guides who show us how to be ourselves by telling us how they managed to be themselves. That is true guidance. That is what a great master does.

In a very early dialogue on the teacher-student relationship, the Buddha said "a good friend, a good teacher, tells you his secrets, and he keeps yours." What works best is transparency—not exhibitionism, but transparency. And transparency always requires some real vulnerability on the part of the teacher. There's no other way.

One of the largest problems confronting modern students seeking a "spiritual" path is the need to idealize teachers, to create imaginary perfection, a sterilized idol, some action figure—a hero dressed in saffron robes instead of a cape or a pirate's mask. This idealization results in the creation of impossible standards against which to judge your own progress. Admiring and looking up to people who have traveled a rugged path and developed hard-won qualities is wonderful. But it's counterproductive to idealize any teacher because you think they don't deal with the same stuff you face. This form of worship renders your own experience foreign to you. I have seen it happen many times. Idealization serves only to distance you from whatever you are studying, because it interrupts your accountability to your own path. The teacher can only tell you of their path. They can't live your life for you.

Sometimes we choose impossible idols (rather than flawed people) to look up to because we actually *want* to remain distant from the path. Waking up is hard work, and if it were possible; who wouldn't want the teacher to do that work for us? If we hold the teacher at a distance through idealization, maybe we can get away from our own trials and tribulations, our own shameful secrets. Waking up requires humanizing the people we look up to, forming a bridge between their wise experience and our own insights waiting to be discovered. Without that human connection, without knowledge of the teacher's own process, anything we learn from them will be like obsessing over a Google Street Map for the planet Jupiter: a detailed description of a place you can't ever visit. This distance doesn't help anyone. What helps are *human examples*. To connect with teachers, we need to be able to ask the questions we really want to ask, not vague, polite ones that elicit more platitudes. Compassion is no platitude. Compassion is just a way to work with a big mess, because compassion flourishes when you feel inclusive of reality, and as long as people exist, reality will be a big mess.

Here are just a few of the questions I have always wanted to ask spiritual teachers:

What is your biggest emotional obstacle?

Who in your family annoys you the most?

Who did you vote for?

If you didn't vote, why the hell not?

Who's your favorite artist?

Have you ever butt-dialed someone?

Have you ever drunk-dialed someone?

Have you ever lied to a friend?

Have you ever felt haunted by a mistake you have yet to fully process?

How do you deal with those moments when you absolutely *hate* your partner?

Or . . . your parents?

Your teacher?

Or those moments when you hate your *children*?

Tell me, wise teacher, tell me of all the self-destructive mistakes you've made, all the obstacles you've faced, all your "clueless" moments on this journey—what did you learn?

When it comes to relationships, as both a teacher and a student, I feel the need to answer these questions myself.

My heroes are imperfect. Yes, they have wisdom, they know their subject thoroughly, but the best teachers are always still learning, and they help us glimpse the invisible bridge between confusion and wisdom. Confusion and wisdom are never completely separate experiences. Rather, they are merely different vantage points of the same human experience. We experience life from both perspectives all the time.

Teachers keep coming back, with deeply good intentions, to their own path, and by their persistence, they give us a glimmer of hope that waking up is something we, too, can do.

Pop Culture Has Become
Our Spiritual Text

WHAT DOES ANY OF THIS have to do with *The Princess Bride*? It just happens to be the spiritual narrative I've chosen to guide me. There are certainly ancient texts one could look to for wisdom, and I look to those repeatedly, but I don't particularly look forward to revisiting them with the same fervor as my favorite movies . . . or art or novels or any other piece of contemporary culture.

Like many other spiritual traditions, Buddhism is, and always has been, about storytelling. So, what is our cultural story? I often use pop and contemporary culture in my lectures. I use art and quote poetry; I reference apps, mention music, and certainly use a *lot* of movie references. It has occurred to me more than a few times that maybe it's irresponsible to reference popular culture in a Buddhist lecture. Perhaps it's a distraction or, even worse, a kind of cultural appropriation. Maybe there isn't much spiritual insight to be found in a popular movie, song, or work of art. Perhaps quoting a line from *The Princess Bride* when I'm talking about karma, or emptiness, while affecting the accent of the Spaniard ("You keep using that word. I do not think it means what you think it means . . ."), is a way to endear myself to an audience in the digital era, a wink of mutually accepted coolness, like a password uttered at the door to a secret nightclub of memes. Maybe this strategy is just a trick of public speaking, a way to earn my students' trust before we get down to the real business of studying ancient teachings on the nature of the mind. Maybe it's wrong to validate a culture shackled by consumerism, a society choking itself and the planet inside a dopamine-infused fog. Maybe people come to meditation precisely because they are suffocating, losing their minds within a digital prison. Maybe we should just turn off all that noise. Maybe I'm fooling myself to pretend that our modern culture has any spiritual value at all.

I believe there's a great deal in our pop culture generally, and in this film in particular, that is spiritually useful. There's just something about this postmodern fairy tale, something about *The Princess Bride*'s rare ability, like a perfect balance of acidic and sweet flavors, to both utterly mock and fully celebrate the genre of which it partakes. The film deconstructs our assumptions about storytelling, but not in the service of the apathy that so many contemporary rearrangements seem to peddle. Rather, this fairy tale, cobbled together from cheesy tropes and sarcastic memes, is offered up in the service of something important, something we can't lose sight of, ever: optimism and, yes, love. True love. And not only true romantic love, but also the true love of one's family and friends. Every time I see this movie, I end up feeling that the love that exists between friends and family is indeed a real thing. This film reminds me that romantic love (even "mawidge"), though it has been commodified, degraded, inflated, repackaged, and misunderstood countless times, is still worth pursuing desperately.

As a teacher, I have noticed again and again that it is when I refer to the stories we share as a society that the Buddhist teachings become most accessible, and my own insights most alive. Today, many of us are as likely to quote something said by Yoda as by Jesus. And from the Baby Boomers onward, Holden Caulfield's story of heroic disillusionment has resonated even more than the origin story of Siddhartha Gautama. Just in the last week of writing this introduction, friends and students have e-mailed me to discuss Buddhist teachings in relationship to: the novels of David Mitchell, the visual art of Kara Walker, the music of Prince and David Bowie, a film by Laurie Anderson, and the comedy of Louis CK.[4] And for the past two decades, people always, always, always want to talk about how totally Buddhist the *Matrix* is, how Morpheus is actually a Buddhist guru.[5] They are far less likely to quote the Dhammapada or even Rumi nowadays. When students are too tired or upset to meditate, few of us pass out while reading Buddhist lectures or yoga sutras. Instead, we might fall down the cultural rabbit hole called Netflix. (As a teacher, I just hope my students get in a little meditation practice before the binge-watching gets under way.) So, in the face of this assault of pop culture, what are we modern practitioners supposed to do?

Culture is everywhere, all the time, and there is no way to become "mindful" outside its grasp. What if we could use our whole cultural experience mindfully, treating our culture as the shared story that helps us all *wake up*, rather than as the lullaby that keeps us dreaming through a dissatisfied and isolated life? It's impossible to pretend that culture isn't influencing our personal narratives, and therefore our privately held thoughts and beliefs, all the time. So if you come to my Buddhism class, I might quote *The*

Princess Bride a few times, usually to immensely positive reception—the story is packed with funny moments, perfect sayings, and potential lessons. In a society where fewer and fewer of us identify as "religious" in any traditional sense, our popular culture, the narratives we have shared from childhood onward, and all the trillions of dollars we have spent and earned sharing them, are now our spiritual texts. In an increasingly nonreligious society, we are stuck with pop culture to guide our spiritual lives.

This approach might anger spiritual purists (though purists, by definition, are easy to anger), but I see its potential to reclaim us from our apathy—to help us become more connected, more compassionate, more equipped to facilitate awakening. Choosing to embrace your world, rather than reject it, is the very essence of enlightened inspiration. If we are going to avoid our wellness practices and hide out in the comfortable crevices of pop culture, then we may as well use that culture, or at least the parts of it that contain brilliance, to help us wake up to reality. After all, every thought you think while you sit in meditation is influenced by the cultural moment you inhabit. What if culture already *is* part of your practice, whether you like it or not? Culture is the air we breathe. Air may be invisible, but that doesn't mean it isn't keeping us alive.

Most often, human beings look to the ancient world for values and principles and to the modern world for narratives that put those values into action. More than any other form of narrative, our movies and television shows are the place where spiritual lessons are learned. Many of these stories teach us cynical lessons: how to be consumers of disposable objects, how to numb ourselves with isolating ideologies that keep us unconcerned about the plight of others. A few rare tales, like *The Princess Bride*, teach us something much more profound: true love *definitely* exists, but not quite the way you think.

Buddhist thought has a special role to play in the updating of storytelling. Buddhism is a tradition based on the context of the present moment, the here and now. For its twenty-five-hundred-year history, Buddhist teachings have relied on dialogue between fellow practitioners, or between teacher and student. The most important teachings in Buddhism utilize examples drawn from the time and place of the people who happen to be its current practitioners. Buddhism has no one core text except for memorized dialogues and instructions, the retold exchanges between students and teachers. Sure, Buddhism has collected bodies of ancient teachings on psychology, ethics, and metaphysics, and these teachings maintain some kind of general orthodoxy. In certain Buddhist traditions, the earliest teachings hold the greatest primacy, especially if those dialogues come from Siddhartha Gautama himself. But even these ancient teachings are conversational, relying on the characters present at that moment, revealing to us what was on their minds. And what was on their minds was based on the culture and society they inhabited. So, even ancient teachings, set in stone or on calligraphed scrolls, as hallowed as they may seem, are nothing but a window onto a specific cultural moment, one captured in time with the purpose of transmitting an insight somehow capable of transcending the moment, of extending toward a more universal human truth. You can't fully convey any ancient teaching without contextualizing the cultural experience of its original audience. Without some understanding of cultural context, no ancient teaching makes much sense. It is context (the who, what, when, where, why, and how of spiritual teaching) that brings the teachings to life and makes them resonate timelessly. They may not have called it "pop culture" in Iron Age India, but you can bet that the Buddha taught absolutely zero outside his cultural and political understanding, zero outside the popular narratives of his own time and place. Siddhartha's story is just one story of awakening. There have been, are, and will be many others.

The people I encounter are generally trying to understand life in the here and now, in this oddly fragmented yet pervasive culture, this strangely globalized world of the twenty-first century in which classic stories (of heroes and villains, good and evil, fear and courage, drama and romcom, verité and fantasy, sci-fi and historical fiction, noir and anime) have been regurgitated, xeroxed, deconstructed, reconstructed, and kept on life support many times over. It has been repeatedly stated that there is no such thing as a new story, that all narrative structures have been exhausted. It is our running out of new stories that gave rise to postmodernity in the first place: the exhaustion of choices regarding how we share human experience. The question for present-day spiritual practitioners is this: How do you tell the story of your spiritual life while living in an era *after* every original story has already been told?

The answer we've come up with collectively is pretty obvious: you don't really tell *new* stories, because, well, you can't. You retell a familiar story in a new context or with a new twist, and hope the retelling is beneficial to everyone. Nobody really seems to care that there's no such thing as a new story. We still fork over the cash and go see a movie with a derivative plot, as long as doing so makes us feel good about the experience. After all, what else are we as humans going to do except share stories, perceptions, memories, insights, and advice?

Meditators learn quickly that there's no such thing as an original thought, either. It's just a lot of the same old recycled material of fear and doubt, love and hate, all re-interpreted for a new moment. If we can't find a new story to tell or a new thought to think, maybe we can learn something we missed the first time around in the many stories already told, those already written and staged and screened. In Buddhism, this sharing of stories, ideas, and practices across generations is known as lineage. According to the Shambhala teachings, if you can't connect with your lineage, then you are truly lost.

The ability to freshly retell a story that has already been told many times is the magic of *The Princess Bride*. Like any Buddhist master, *The Princess Bride* is self-aware, and also aware of its era. It knows exactly what it is: a postmodern fairy tale, a fairy tale that exists after the exhaustion of all fairy-tale possibilities, after all fantasies have long ago been told. *The Princess Bride* also knows that true love is exhausted, and the fantasy version of love is, well, full of crap. One of the primary features of our cynical era is that we don't easily worship any idealistic version of romance anymore. This loss of heart about true love makes us halfway numb and halfway fixated on instant gratification, which is a recipe for unhappiness.

An "Awake-ist" story must do something ironic. It must deconstruct false views, but in the end, it must also recover optimism for those who share the story. A good Awake-ist fantasy—and that's what I believe *The Princess Bride* is— will make you fall deeper in love with the world as it is. It will make you plug yourself back into the rugged beauty of reality, so that you will want to protect *this* imperfect world more, and protect the imperfect beings who live here. For the Awake-ist, a good fantasy leads you back to now with a renewed sense of compassion.

When it comes to relationships, no pop culture story has been more my companion over the years than *The Princess Bride*. What follows are insights and blunders I've collected in a life spent trying to be a basically good Buddhist kid and eventually a basically good Buddhist man, a man attempting to wake up to himself and help others. Yes, it is ironic that I need to discuss a fairy tale to tell you what I know of love in the real world. May it be of benefit to those nostalgic romantics, glued to our screens, still trying desperately to wake up.

PART I

THE DHARMA OF FRIENDSHIP

Inigo looked at [Fezzik]. "You mean you'll forgive me completely for saving your life if I completely forgive you for saving mine?"

"You're my friend, my only one," [Fezzik said].

"Pathetic, that's what we are," Inigo said.

—FROM *THE PRINCESS BRIDE*, BY WILLIAM GOLDMAN

Mercenaries or Besties

What Are Friends For?

OBEY FEZZIK.

When Andre the Giant's stenciled face began appearing everywhere in American cities in the 1990s, immortalized against brick and concrete in the artist Shepard Fairey's series of "OBEY" stickers, posters, and graffiti, his image suddenly became Americana. Before his death in 1993, and before the generational rise of this movie, Andre the Giant was best known as an angry, hulking, powerful professional wrestler. But I was way more interested in his character from *The Princess Bride*, Fezzik. I used to imagine that the face depicted on Fairey's authoritarian stencils was not the 7-foot, 4-inch, 520-pound World Wrestling Federation icon. Instead, these drawings were asking me to "OBEY" Fezzik.

If you visualized Fezzik, then Fairey's work was no longer a clever send-up of an Orwellian theme. "OBEY" was, instead, a gentle reminder, a soft demand from Fezzik for loyalty and friendship, a command I was happy to follow. The WWF persona was a man to fear, the kind of giant who might throw you off a cliff if you triggered his wrath. Not Fezzik. Fezzik was on my side, your side, *our* side. Not just some colossus, Fezzik was a tenderhearted poet ("Anybody want a peanut?"), the kind of comrade who would carry you and several friends up the sheerest of cliffs, even the Cliffs of Insanity; or who would nurse you back to health from your brandy-amplified PTSD; or who would bring you four perfect horses exactly when you needed them to make sure you got away safely, reaching a place where no bad guys could ever find you. Fezzik was the friend of all friends.

The Princess Bride is, first and foremost, a story of friendship. More specifically, it is a story of loners who finally find their real pals. It tells of an unforeseen "bromance," one of the greatest bromances ever to inhabit the silver screen. Their friendship begins with a post-traumatic, mercenaries-turned-besties alliance between the Turkish giant Fezzik and the Spaniard Inigo Montoya. This partnership later includes Westley, the Farmboy turned Dread Pirate Roberts turned back into Westley again. These three unlikely friends overcome their personal demons to support each other's journeys in grief, revenge, and, of course, storming the castle to liberate the Princess. Like most friendships, theirs is a beautiful accident of circumstance, a harmonizing of shared suffering, a camaraderie that is only just beginning when the story ends.

Friendship is never a guarantee. In this story, each hero begins as a loner. In the book version, the karmic origins of their solitude are further examined. Fezzik and Inigo have come together as mercenaries, and are already close friends when the movie begins, but their origin stories mark them both as social outcasts who each lost their parents too soon. Inigo's mother died in childbirth, and his father was brutally murdered by the Six-Fingered Man, leaving Inigo alone at the tender age of eleven. In the book, Fezzik loses his parents inexplicably during a young wrestling career in Mongolia. Westley's origin is never clearly established, only that he works in squalor as some kind of serf for the family of his beloved Buttercup. And as the Man in Black, it's obvious Westley prefers to roll solo. So why do these heroes come together? What's in it for them?

What's in it for *anyone*? Why do we ever befriend each other? Is there a biological or spiritual imperative to friendship? Do comrades aid our spiritual journey, or are we better off, as many spiritual voices have modeled and taught over the ages, figuring life out in solitude? Perhaps our desire for friendship is a remnant of our tribal days, when we had to team up to defend ourselves against neighboring clans. Thus our ancestors passed along the habit of identifying with a tight band of comrades, of defining a "we," of forming a posse, a squad to help us survive a dangerous world.

The haphazard origin of the friendships among the characters in *The Princess Bride* brings to mind the accidental origin of most friendships. Few friendships are ever planned. Your friends start as the kid your mother made you play with when you were little (exactly how my father became best friends with the Six-Fingered Man), the girl who sat down next to you in the university cafeteria as you faced doubts about your self-worth in an unfamiliar social setting, the guy you found yourself in a heated political conversation with at a cousin's wedding reception, the woman with whom you commiserated on the torment of having the same horrible boss, the one you kept bumping into in creative circles and with whom you eventually exchanged contact information. Friendship has something to do with coincidence, but also with mutual benefit. Friends find each other through attraction, but the chemistry involved is much harder to name than sexual or romantic longing. We can't be sure why Fezzik and Inigo, for example, love each other so dearly, but their *Odd Couple* charm reminds me of the pull of so many friendships over the course of my own life.

Inigo and Fezzik meet as mercenaries working under a man who is the definition of a bad boss, the Sicilian "genius" Vizzini. Perhaps the two create bad karma when they help Vizzini with his plot to kidnap and kill Buttercup. However, as the story makes clear, the two are good guys who've lost their parents and might just exhibit poor judgment when it comes to obeying their abusive employer.

Lose your parents, find an abusive new father figure. It's a classic story. When we meet them, Inigo and Fezzik have built an amazing connection, a friendship that will eventually include a third, heartbroken warrior, the formerly innocent Farmboy Westley, now the deft Man in Black, aka the current holder of the title "Dread Pirate Roberts." Personally, I always longed to be part of such a wacky brotherhood, or brother-and-sisterhood, and turned to this movie whenever my life felt as if it were missing the presence of that genuine quirky and supportive friend. Whenever I couldn't find my Fezzik in real life, I found Fezzik here.

Meditation:
First, Make Friends with Yourself

PARTICIPATING IN A GREAT FRIENDSHIP is one of the wonders of life. How do you find one? Are there clear Buddhist rules for when a friendship is at its best, when it aids one's practice of mindfulness and compassion? From a Buddhist perspective, a good friendship is one that helps you recall your awakened qualities, qualities that, like muscles, need to be developed through training. These qualities include patience, generosity, and insight.

There are certainly some classic Buddhist guidelines for building healthy friendships. But to understand the Buddhist approach to friendship, you have to start at the beginning. The key to friendship, to finding your Fezzik, is first to make friends with yourself. There is a simple word for this process of accepting your own friend request: that word is *meditation*.[1] In the Shambhala tradition, meditation has nothing to do with leaving the world behind or transcending anything. It has to do with getting to know yourself so that you will be poised to befriend others more fully.

Those who meditate will tell you that meditation brings you more in touch with your aloneness. Mindfulness delivers an experience of the mind that cannot be directly shared by anyone else. Meditation can provoke a lot of restlessness and, on a deeper level, unveil anxiety and fear because the practice points out the raw truth, stripped bare of distractions, that you are, in fact, always alone with your own mind.

The mind that is discovered in meditation is a personal and private space, a movie theater with a seating capacity of one. I often joke that we should serve ourselves popcorn during meditation sessions, because the mind is history's greatest cinema. Sit up, relax, and enjoy the show. Sometimes my personal movie is boring, like watching twenty minutes of C-SPAN. At other times, my mind is more rambunctious, like an episode of *Game of Thrones*. In the theater of self-awareness, you are cowriter, codirector, and audience for your own perceptions, beliefs, and opinions. If you don't believe me, put down this book, sit tall, and for a few minutes just watch your thoughts dance. Don't worry about finding the breath (or any other meditation technique you may have encountered). Just let your awareness go wherever your thoughts lead you. Even if you're bored, there's actually quite a compelling movie being shown in there—or in "here," or wherever the mental theater actually "is."

Something seminal happened to me during that same difficult era when I discovered *The Princess Bride*. I took my first formal class in meditation, a class just for children. I was nine or ten, and found the practice incredibly boring—I didn't start meditating semi-regularly until high school—but it was a productive boredom, a nonevent that carried tremendous value. Being silent with the tools of mindfulness introduced me to a feeling of vivid ordinariness. In that space, the seeds were planted for a delayed-release curiosity about the mind. Most of the ordinary magic of meditation was lost on me at the time—I fell in love with the practice only later on—but I remember the value of realizing that I had an entire internal world to explore, my own VHS collection of thoughts and stories, perceptions and projections.

The mind was an inner space that was related to, and yet totally distinct from, the world out there. In fact, my mind was my true home, a home into which others could never be fully invited. Because of this privacy, the mind is a realm equal parts scary and fascinating: one part castle, one part haunted house. I have spent many years since then trying to get to know my mind a bit better, in order to become more genuinely available for the people I know and love.

As I've said, if you're going to learn how to befriend other humans, you have to match that effort by befriending yourself. In the course of my life, if I really wanted to "find my people," I also had to learn how to find myself, if not as my best friend then at least as my *first* friend. Later on, the existential confusions of puberty and high school made me commit to regular meditation. And the first time I got dumped in college, that's when I knew I was a Buddhist. During those years, the practice and teachings became indispensable to who I was.

When you meditate, you don't find instantaneous peace, although practice can definitely guide you into a less tumultuous inner setting, a relative calm within body and mind, at least temporarily. The positive effects of mindfulness techniques on the parasympathetic nervous system have been well documented, both anecdotally and empirically. I trust the accumulated accounts of millions of practitioners more than I trust the objective evidence of scientific studies, but both are quite helpful.

There is, however, one big fairy tale currently being offered up about meditation: the fantasy of transcendence, the possibility of entering a permanent bliss state, an inner paradise devoid of thoughts and feelings. Some systems of meditation promise a sudden bypassing of all the discomfort of thoughts and emotions, the ability to settle into the same induced ease every single time you sit. While these approaches may have some positive effects on stress levels, I believe they are not as reliable as promised. And even if these versions of meditation are helpful, they miss the real treasure chest of the practice. The deepest benefit of meditation, for me, is the possibility of befriending the inherent creativity of the mind itself. When you feel at home in your awareness *as it is*, you have access to the power of your mind as a creative tool. The mind no longer needs to be wrestled or suppressed into peace. When your awareness is like a movie screen, and your thoughts are seen as worthy characters, the mind becomes like a theater. When you watch a movie, would you rather get to know the characters or pretend they don't exist?

Genuine meditation includes a certain amount of discomfort. Chief among the uncomfortable experiences of meditation, you will eventually discover, are your own Rodents of Unusual Size. In this case, they are Rodents of Unusually *Small* Size, so small they aren't even physical entities. These Rodents of Unusually Small Size are negative thoughts, the aggressive commentaries with endless self-critiques that gnaw at you. They're the thoughts that tell you you aren't good enough, not properly equipped to be human. These pests try to convince you that you're probably going to die forgotten and unloved. As I began to practice more throughout my teenage years, I saw that I had a seemingly endless supply of these mental rodents scurrying around. No one knows yet where negative thoughts reside physically in brain or body, or where they come from—they aren't single origin. Maybe it's our advertising culture that forces these Rodents of Unusually Small Size upon us; maybe it's institutional racism and sexism; maybe it's inherited trauma from our parental and genetic lineages regarding self-worth; maybe it's an inheritance from a previous lifetime of confused circumstances. I think it might just be all of the above. Who knows?

Long before anyone knew what the brain looked like or how a nervous system functioned, the Buddha realized an important point. Moment by moment, we don't need to know exactly where our thoughts live in the brain; we just need to know how to work with them. The set of tools for doing so could collectively be called "mindfulness." Over time, mindfulness can help you cohabitate your nervous system safely with the Rodents of an Unusually Small Size. With greater familiarity, some of your negative thoughts might become harmless. Some rodents might dissolve into space. Some might even morph into little Mice of Compassion.

Embracing Aloneness

THE PURPOSE OF MEDITATION IS to learn to be truly yourself. But if you want to be yourself, you have to invest considerable training in being *with* yourself. As I have discovered through my own struggles, if you don't set aside time for getting to know your mind directly, then in the presence of others your sense of self will get increasingly confused. Without mindfulness, you will always be constructing your sense of self based on others' perceptions. Why is this externalized experience of self a problem? Because you can't ever really know for sure what others think of you. You receive only occasional feedback: gestures, glances, comments about who people think you are. These external messages are always subjective, momentary, and indirect, received in pieces, brief exchanges, fragments of interaction.

So without being able to *know* what others think of you, you are left to define your sense of self in terms of what you *believe* others *might* think about you, which is two degrees of separation from a verified connection with your own mind. Meanwhile, while you worry what others think, they are caught up in the same game themselves, worrying what you think of them. A friendship between two people without self-awareness is like trying to talk to somebody standing right next to you by calling them on a cell phone with only one bar of reception. You try to say hello, sending a signal to a satellite many miles above, and you wait for the weak signal to ricochet back. The other person, standing next to you, speaks into their own phone, and the message goes to space and back before reappearing in your ear, garbled, indecipherable. You think to yourself, "Did they just say something mean about me? I bet they did." Without mindfulness practice, this is what our sense of self often feels like: indirect, chaotic, and full of gnawing assumptions about the unclear messages we receive from others.

On top of this indirect experience of self, we often operate from the premise that the messages we receive confirm an underlying suspicion: that there is something fundamentally wrong with us. In a society where the residual belief in original sin is deeply embedded in our secular identity, suspicion of human nature is the cultural air we all inhale. If you assume that your humanity is somehow flawed, unwholesome, or broken, then you might fear that time spent with others will expose this underlying brokenness. If you engage in friendships from this angle, you will always be relating to friends while hoping to fix the things about yourself that you're afraid the other person sees. Now you're several degrees and one big Pit of Despair away from experiencing yourself directly. The solution to this mess is not to abandon other people; it's to give befriending yourself the same urgency that you give to befriending others.

The Shambhala teachings are based on a radical view about the nature of all human beings, and all sentient beings. Nothing at all is broken; wisdom is the deepest stitching in the very fabric of consciousness. This optimistic view of the nature of all sentient beings is often referred to as *basic goodness.*

The word *goodness* often confuses people. It is not meant to place a value judgment on either people or experiences, as if some were good and some bad. Yes, some people, more than others, might be ruled by destructive views and harmful habits. But in the context of mindfulness, the word *good* lacks any sense of evaluation or comparison to some other object that is deemed better or worse. Instead, it refers to appreciation without comparison. *Good* here simply means worthy of existing, worthy of being experienced.

In the Shambhala teachings, enlightenment refers to a person who remains fully connected to their basic goodness at all times, completely relaxing into the confidence that such a spacious sense of self-worth carries with it. An awake person can handle anything life throws at them: pain and pleasure, successes and letdowns, confusion and wisdom, depression and elation, even birth and death.

The reason meditation has meant so much to me is that I have come to see it entirely as my daily preparation for relationships. Every good relationship is based on the willingness of each participant first to be alone. When it comes to experiencing your own mind, you are always alone, and you could find natural strength in this aloneness, rather than viewing it as some state of desperation needing to be fixed or healed by another person. Buddhist teacher Ajahn Sumedho says it like this: "When it comes to the actual experience of life, we are very much alone; and to expect anyone else to take away our loneliness is asking too much." Sitting in the movie theater of your mind, you are alone. Others have cocreated the spectacle, but you are the only one who bought a ticket for this private screening.

That being said, we still need a means of sharing our lives, even if the act of sharing aloneness can only ever be an approximation. This is where the human need for art and culture originates, why the relationship between mindfulness and culture is so important. Culture is the collective language of personal experiences. Throughout the ages, humans have invented all forms of it: music, visual arts, architecture, storytelling, poetry, and fairy tales, all to share what it is like to be a unique perceiving, feeling, thinking person. Culture is our best method for being alone together.

Introverts Unite!

A FAVORITE T-SHIRT OF MINE boasts the rallying cry "Introverts Unite! We're Here! We're Uncomfortable! And We Want to Go Home!" I love this T-shirt because it points to the boundaries of our solitude and the parameters of our interconnection.

Those who have studied the nature of human consciousness deeply—whether approaching it from the standpoint of psychology, spirituality, sociology, or biology—have had to deal with a riddle, a seemingly irresolvable tension. This question is at the core of any contemporary interpretation of Buddhist teachings. It involves how personal experience interacts with social experience. On the one hand, we each rely on other people constantly. None of us is self-sufficient, at least not in the external world. Our physical realities occur in a fluid state of molecular and causal interdependence.

Interdependence is not only about the physics of the outer world. Your inner world, your very personal and private state of mind, is also entirely shaped by the influence of others. There are more than seven billion humans on this planet now, creating a precarious network of interdependent cultures and views. From the start of life in the womb, your sense of self is affected and molded by attachment and by relationships to those who are not you, especially those who nurture you, or fail to nurture you; to those who instill feelings of safety and belonging. As the Zen master Thich Nhat Hanh points out, whatever is Me is always molded by that which is Not Me. A flower, he famously contends, is made up of nonflower elements: the sun, the soil, the water, and especially the human minds that decided on the strange label *daffodil*. Without all these nonflower influences, a flower couldn't be a flower. Even our bodies are not all "us." Nine-tenths are composed of foreign microbes. Quite literally, 90 percent of you is *not* you. Even those of us who claim to be independent have learned how to be independent by following the lead of people we admire. In terms of cause and effect, declaring our "independence" is literally a joke.

Modern neuroscience tells us that our brains operate in a social manner, as our nervous systems are primed to take cues from the nervous systems of those around us. As the neuroscientist David Eagleman says, "Brains have traditionally been studied in isolation, but that approach overlooks the fact that an enormous amount of brain circuitry has to do with *other* brains. We are deeply social creatures. All this social glue is generated by specific circuitry in the brain: sprawling networks that monitor other people, communicate with them, feel their pain, judge their intentions, and read their emotions. Our social skills are deeply rooted in our neural circuitry—and understanding this circuitry is the basis of a young field of study called social neuroscience."[2]

This "young" field of study called social neuroscience can join together with an ancient field of study called Mahayana Buddhism, a group of contemplative traditions that could be translated as the practice of "relational awakening." Honoring this social, interconnected nature of life is every bit as important to our awakening as self-inquiry and personal accountability might be. Scientists also believe that the longing to connect deeply with others is what distinguishes the most advanced part of our brains from the brains of earlier mammals and reptiles. What makes us different from salamanders, squirrels, and early primates is our deep, unstoppable longing to link up with each other, our karmic wiring for connectivity.[3] Even in our most analytical moments of abstract philosophy, we are still seeking contact with other humans. If Buddhism is about living an awakened life, then we must be aware of our need for genuine connection as the basis for that human awakening.

Even classical Buddhist teachings are completely based on reliance on others, a fact that sometimes gets missed in the more individualistic interpretations of the Buddhist paradigm. We are each asked to contemplate the meaning of *sangha*, the community of friends or peers who share our journey through life, those who give us the power to become more mindful and compassionate.

Whether we believe we are supposed to rely on others or to go it alone comes from the stories we inherit from our culture. *The Princess Bride* starts out as a classic American loner tale, but soon morphs into a story of total reliance on friends. At first glance, the Man in Black (Westley in disguise) might seem the perfect libertarian hero, more so than even a solitary yogi like the Buddha. When we first meet him, he seems to have gotten used to working alone, via his pirate training. Working alone has gotten him pretty far in the story, and it has made him look exceptionally cool. Within the American canon of powerful superhero loners, the Man in Black is akin to Batman's younger, wittier (and much poorer) brother. But even this superhero needs the help of friends, and Westley can't get his true love back, or even survive his own plot, without their help.

When you sit alone in meditation, you start to realize that, amazingly, you were never alone, because you see clearly that you didn't write your own script. We have to balance the experience of our aloneness with the truth of just how interdependently constructed we are.[4] Here is the tension we each must inhabit, a tension that perhaps describes all

Buddhist teachings: Your sense of self can only be experienced personally, but it is constructed socially. If we understand this tension, we will understand reality. With this insight, what once was a friction between the twin truths of aloneness and interdependence melts into harmony. The parallel practices of making friends with yourself and making friends with others begin to complement each other. Time spent in solitude and time spent with others can each help you awaken. At last, an introvert has no choice but to accept their interdependence with others, at least if they want to understand reality fully. And it is exactly at this point that good friendships become crucial for any spiritual path, that moment when introverts realize we must unite.

What Is a "Good" Friend?

SOMETIMES IT'S ABUNDANTLY CLEAR HOW the right friends bring out the best spiritual qualities in us—if we'd only pay attention. Once upon a time, I was living with a close friend in Brooklyn. This friend was exceptionally thoughtful and compassionate. At the time, he was my Westley in body, my Fezzik in spirit, and my passionate Inigo if I ever needed a verbal swordsman to defend me against attacks from others. One day we discovered that our apartment had a mouse problem (Rodents of the *Usual* Size). My friend said he would buy traps, and I automatically assumed he would get those nondeadly traps. I didn't know much about mouse traps; I remembered only an incident years earlier, when my mother and I caught a mouse in a humane trap and walked pleasantly to a nearby park to set it free. This rosy memory might've engrained in me the assumption that anybody I considered a compassionate person would always use nondeadly traps. A few days after my friend set the traps out, I came home before him to find that we'd indeed caught a mouse. I examined the helpless creature, recently caught, stuck on a tray of glue that it had mistaken for an oasis of cheese and honey. I could see its tiny lungs heaving anxiously for breath. For a moment, I mirrored the mouse's pain, that pain we all know: the trauma of blindly mistaking entrapment for safety— confusing "ouch" for "wow"—the suffering born of not knowing how to navigate this cosmos without getting yourself caught up in a horrific situation. I scratched my head, trying to figure out how to liberate the mouse from this have-a-heart trap that my have-a-heart friend had laid for it, in his indisputably have-a-heart manner.

I brought the tray out onto the fire escape and started trying to work the mouse free from the glue. Its legs were stuck, and the glue seemed *extra* sticky. The mouse kept trying to bite my hands, but I kept working, eventually getting one leg out of the glue, then another. Honestly, I was close to giving up, assuming the trap had simply malfunctioned. I considered secretly hurling the mouse off the fire escape so that it would die as quickly as possible, but I couldn't let my best friend down. How could I look him in the eye if I gave up and killed the mouse? Would I have to lie to him? I couldn't abide these thoughts. After about twenty minutes of careful work, I finally freed the little torso, and the mouse limped away and disappeared. When my friend came home a little later, I told him that we had caught a mouse. "Did you . . . um . . . kill it?" he asked, cautiously. "Of course not!" I said, still clueless. "It took me like twenty minutes to free the little dude."

My friend suddenly hugged me deeply, like Amma might. "Oh, man, you are *so* sweet. The hardware store was out of humane traps, and those don't really work anyway. I mean, I wish they worked, but . . . oh, man. You're just supposed to crush it with something heavy and put it out of its misery as fast as you can."

I tried to tell my friend that I had kept going with my rodent liberation project to look good in his eyes. One classic Buddhist teaching on compassion states it very simply: "With some [friends], your shortcomings fade away and your positive abilities grow like the waxing moon. Hold such [friends] dear to you, dearer than your own body."[5]

It was only because I'd assumed my friend was compassionate that I chose the hard work of doing the right thing for that creature. At other times, I have done the wrong thing simply because no one was around to help me raise the bar for my conduct, or because I was unable to follow the guidance of those who had tried. The world is composed of both stories. On the one hand, we all have those fourth-grade stories, the "no-clue" narratives enacted out of confusion, when no one is around to inspire you to do that which is skillful, that which is kind. On the other hand, you can celebrate the stories of a friend going above and beyond the call of duty and inspiring you to be more awake than you would otherwise have been. That kind of friend makes all the difference.

My teacher Sakyong Mipham Rinpoche has repeatedly made the same case: it matters whom you invite into your personal sphere. He calls it "hanging out with the right crowd." He's not talking about the cool kids. He's talking about associating with those people who help you wake up. In my R.O.U.S. story, I was grateful to have a well-chosen friend, because our friendship made me raise my compassion game, so to speak. In fact, a Buddhist definition for *best friend* could simply be the person who helps you bring out your "best" qualities: mindfulness, generosity, patience, confidence, and creativity. The best friends are the ones who support your awakening, and whose awakening you in turn support.

Discernment vs. Judgment: Letting Go of the Wrong Friendships

GIVEN THAT MOST FRIENDSHIPS BEGIN by coincidence, how do you choose your friends? In that same classic Buddhist text on compassion, the one that tells you to spend as much time as possible with those who bring out your highest qualities, well, just a few verses later, it says the opposite. It says you should work with difficult people with an open heart, treating even your toughest relationships as sacred teachers, because difficult people can reveal opportunities for you to develop patience and generosity. How do we reconcile these two statements, the need to be careful about whom you create a close friendship with, and the need to welcome difficult people as potential teachers? For anyone trying to be both mindful and compassionate, this dilemma may lead to a codependent relationship or feeling like a doormat.

The Buddhist ideal of a *bodhisattva* complicates the practice of friendship. A bodhisattva is a being who dedicates their existence to the benefit of many others. Students of Buddhism are eventually invited to take on such an aspiration themselves. Just how many "others" are we talking about? The classic teachings on becoming a bodhisattva say the student should dedicate their life to *all* beings. This number is so vast, and such an abstraction, that it's hard to pinpoint its meaning. Yet the teachings are unanimous in declaring that happiness comes from working to benefit as many others as one possibly can. Personally, I can't even begin to conceptualize the simultaneously microscopic and intergalactic nature of this request. Our inability to conceptualize the bodhisattva's aspiration is part of its power. But this ideal also brings up an important question about accountability to other beings. Am I supposed to perform the same duties for all beings that I would for a close friend? Am I supposed to help all sentient beings move a heavy couch up two flights of stairs?

The answer lies in the definition of *friend*. Friendship is a special relationship; your close friends represent something very different from someone you simply care about. You can care about many beings, including tremendously difficult or disturbed people, but you can exist in an active relationship with only a limited number of friends. Each time we choose to cultivate a friendship with someone, we are making an important choice.

A crucial concept in Tibetan Buddhism is the idea that each of us lives within the intimacy of something called a *mandala*, a Sanskrit word meaning "sacred circle." In the Shambhala teachings, we use the mandala as an artistic mapping of the close relationships that comprise our life, family, colleagues, close friends, and life partners. A friend once referred to the mandala as a depiction of a personal ecosystem. Visually, a mandala is a depiction of all the supportive relationships that help you fulfill your intention to wake up.

Social media greatly complicates the definition of personal relationships, because it stretches the boundaries of your personal ecosystem far beyond anything humans (and human nervous systems) have been able to keep track of before. In some ways, the technology of our era is wonderful for compassion, because we can bear witness to the lives of more people than ever before. Isn't it amazing that everybody you knew in the fourth grade, everyone you were mean to, and vice versa, can now find you again?

By training the mind, you can develop compassion for all beings, but you can't carry everyone up the Cliffs of Insanity. Even Facebook, perhaps in the interest of avoiding virtual "compassion fatigue," limits the number of friends we can each accept. If you can choose a few good friends to inhabit your life, that might just be enough. The only way to avoid feeling like a total failure as a friend is to choose carefully whom you want to associate with, and practice those relationships with a clarified intention. This requires understanding that there's no such thing as bad people, but there is such a thing as bad friendship.

Perhaps the term *bad friendship* sounds judgmental. In Buddhism, judgment and nonjudgment are very often misunderstood. (It often seems that Buddhists aren't supposed to have an opinion, or even make choices, but you can't avoid making choices in life—about where to shop, whom to vote for, how to decorate your bedroom, and especially whom to associate with.) *Nonjudgmental* means allowing experiences, especially potentially painful ones, to enter your heart and mind. A judgmental attitude is neither scientific nor kind. With judgment, you neglect to let the moment even touch you. Before you're aware of what's happening you've already passed a verdict, so you can't see clearly. Friendship requires the ability to differentiate between healthy and unhealthy, quinoa and cocaine (or worse, iocane). You can remain completely nonjudgmental toward drug addiction, but that doesn't mean that you want to get addicted yourself. Some friendships simply aren't healthy.

To take an example from *The Princess Bride*, Wallace Shawn gives us the gift of Vizzini, one of the best bad friends in cinematic history. He is a particularly poor choice to befriend when you are suffering the way Inigo and Fezzik are both suffering—from the trauma of losing their parents at an early age. Vizzini is that bad friend who promises shelter and sustenance but instead delivers abuse and misdirection. I'm sure we've all been in an unfortunate friendship like that or had a boss like him (and I'm sure the boss wasn't nearly as funny as Vizzini). Maybe you've even followed a spiritual teacher like Vizzini, an emotional puppeteer who berated and gaslighted you constantly, making you live in a constant state of fear that if you didn't give him what he wanted, you'd end up unemployed in Greenland, or otherwise discarded, drowning in dangerous waters.

Bad friendships don't support the development of mindfulness, and they incubate our worst qualities: insecurity, escapism, and jealousy. Unhealthy friendships are founded on the belief that we are okay only if someone else tells us we are okay, which is quite a tenuous definition of safety. At their worst, bad friendships are paralyzing rituals of codependence that enable our worst qualities to stay frozen over a long period of time.

A relationship that undercuts confidence in your basic goodness can make it harder for you ever to want to develop mindfulness. Mindfulness can only grow in an environment where there is a yearning to be present. But if you are surrounded only by people who make you feel basically bad about yourself, why wouldn't you want to escape the present moment, and even escape your own body, every chance you got? It might be wise to exercise caution when you let someone into your mandala, your personal ecosystem. If you are going to expand your capacity to help others, those close to you need to participate in a structure that's supportive for your awakening, and you need to return the favor to them.

Ironically, the more nonjudgmental you become, the more discerning you get about whether to cultivate a closer friendship with a given person. "Nonjudgment" is the clarity you need to see that some relationships just don't work. The difference between a healthy and an unhealthy friendship is not whether you love each other; it's whether you help each other wake up. And if two people want to help each other awaken, they need to do something that the greatest action movies of our time understand. To help each other wake up, you have to help each other beat the bad guys.

The Bad Guys

Out There vs. in Here

HOW DOES A BUDDHIST RECONCILE THE NASTIER parts of *The Princess Bride*, the fencing and torture, the poison and vengeance? Never mind the comedy—how can a Buddhist embrace all that violence? Inigo Montoya has spent most of his life, since the age of eleven, hunting down his father's killer, the Six-Fingered Man. In the process, he's become a master swordsman, learning every known technique of fencing, with both hands. In order to avenge his father's death, he must help his new friend Westley dispatch his own main foe, the power-mad and greedy Prince Humperdinck, who stands in the way of Westley's loving reunion with Buttercup. But before that, Westley must free his new friends from the mentally abusive grasp of Vizzini, the deluded Sicilian who fancies himself a genius. (Despite his arrogant delusions, Vizzini is right about one thing: land wars in Asia do take a lot out of you.) There is little in this story that can be directly considered peaceful.

The fantasy plot of *The Princess Bride* is a humorous collision of revenge narrative and romantic fairy tale, which means it includes bad guys, violence, and, yes, death: the deaths of two bad guys, along with the humiliation of a third. What, if anything, could possibly be Buddhist about revenge? So many modern scripts are driven by simplistic quests, with cookie-cutter plots regurgitating the troubling idea of "an eye for an eye." By any standard, revenge is a confused act because it does not heal the initial wrong it seeks to resolve; it only perpetuates the cycle of violence. It's simple math: vengeance does not equalize the wrongdoing; instead, it doubles it. As they trudge along, revenge narratives become anticlimactic, like a deflating balloon, because there's simply no reason to care. You know how this will end, almost every time. It's not clear whether such narratives could contain insight from a Buddhist perspective. At last, the spiritual usefulness of such a story depends on what you mean by "enemy," and what it means to defeat one.

At the very least, *The Princess Bride* produces something that many unaware revenge tales fail to achieve:

evildoers who are also funny. Villains imbued with humor, rather than terror, tend to remind us less and less of someone "out there" and more and more of ourselves. A funny bad guy makes a more inviting mirror for observing our own obstacles and shortcomings. When we start to examine the nature of villains, it leads to an often clichéd spiritual question: Are there really bad guys "out there," or are enemies just a projection of our own inner obstacles, of those rough states of mind we haven't learned to deal with yet?

Often, in the pursuit of humility, classic spiritual teachings focus attention on internalized enemies. Following an ethos of introspection, these arguments assure us that all our ideas of good and evil are nothing but a projection of our own consciousnesses. Enemies, they suggest, are merely reflections of those things we don't like about ourselves. "Look within. *Only* look within. Just *keep* looking within. The world is not coming *toward* you. It is coming *from* you. You can only work on yourself. Don't worry so much about what others might do." This statement comes from belief in a sort of radical accountability, and proposes that the individual mind is *entirely* responsible for its own experience of reality.

Meditation's primary purpose is indeed to look within, offering tools that help us observe how we have disempowered ourselves by externalizing the causes of happiness. We often move through life putting our joy in the hands of others. This wish puts tremendous pressure on the external world to give us what we want. But the world will only occasionally deliver on our desires. On the other hand, we think our happiness is impeded because external enemies are standing in the way: "Those crazy people over there are stopping me from getting work, or creative recognition, or true love."

This argument for personal responsibility contains great truth, but its context is incomplete. Just look around you: Of course there are bad guys in the outer world! Anybody who has ever had a demeaning boss, or survived a manipulative relationship, or lived in a country ruled by an unelected tyrant, can tell you that our obstacles are not only internal, although our experience of them is certainly personal. Our world is full of oppression, and it's just not equal; some people hold more power and privilege in making it so. How cruel and damaging would it be to tell a slave that all he has to do is look within, without holding slave masters and the system of slavery accountable for their horrific deeds?

The Shambhala tradition refers to internal obstacles—hang-ups like jealousy, obsession, pride, self-doubt—as "enemies." This surprising wording allows us to create a needed link between inner demons and outer bad guys. Meanwhile, practitioners refer to ourselves as "warriors" on a path toward conquering confusion, both within ourselves and in the world. *Warriors* and *enemies*—embedded in the Buddhist vocabulary is its own sort of fantasy narrative, a twist of language that lets you call upon the same feeling of courage embedded in heroic myths.

Perhaps our biggest challenge today is recognizing that evil isn't a description of a person but of a repeated behavior, habitual actions rising from confusion. More than a few reality-challenged, compassion-deficient men like Vizzini,

Count Rugen, and Humperdinck have risen to political power in the decades since this movie came into the world. The results of their empowerment have not been nearly as funny as the events in the film. When a war against Guilder is plotted upon a totally made-up premise, it's quite funny. When a war against Iraq is plotted upon a totally made-up premise, it's not funny at all.

In the world of storytelling, a comedic bad guy momentarily takes the edge off our need to solve all the ills of the world we inhabit. A funny villain gives us a gentle mirror for looking within, at the bad guys inside.

The Enemies Within

OFTEN, A SENSE OF HUMOR is exactly what gives us the bravery required for self-examination. In order to spot the internal bad guys, we need to witness them as characters, to give them voices and personas that embody afflicted states of mind. In this way, comedic bad guys serve a dual purpose. On the one hand, they offer some cathartic pleasure, a needed oasis from which to assess the "real" bad guys who inhabit the world in which we live. On the other hand, comedy reflects back to us our own inner enemies. For me, it is important to have a list of favorite fictional "bad guys," such as the three in *The Princess Bride*. Their vices give me the space to label my own confusion without vilifying myself. We are each Humperdinck every time our greed gets the best of us; we are each Vizzini every time we pretend to know something we simply don't; and we are each the Six-Fingered Man, Rugen, every time we take just a bit too much sordid pleasure in another being's suffering.

The point is not to destroy your enemies; that would be like crushing your own organs in an attempt to cure a disease. Instead, you work to see how the enemy inside (such as greed) can be acknowledged, observed, and gradually disarmed. Maybe you can even transform the enemy's energy into a new kind of ally, the way that the self-enriching focus of greed can turn into the collective-enriching focus of generosity, the way hatred can reveal patience, the way anxiety can become courage.

If you choose good friends who can help you spot your own inner enemies, you might gain the insight necessary to confront and disarm the bad guys you meet in real life. If I understand my own self-centered reactions, for example, I might gain insight into dealing with a narcissistic or grandiose boss. If I understand my tendency to fill up silent spaces, a need to perform during social events, then I can develop empathy for a friend who just won't stop talking. If I understand my own need to be validated, I might gain insight into someone else's arrogance and entitlement.

This movie isn't explicitly a Buddhist story. But if there is any theme in *The Princess Bride* that dovetails perfectly with Buddhist teachings, it's that of the three bad guys: Vizzini, Count Rugen, and Prince Humperdinck. The three villains in this movie map beautifully onto the three core "enemies" that classic Buddhism repeatedly addresses: delusion, hatred, and greed.[1] Vizzini is the embodiment of delusion (also translated as ignorance), Rugen represents hatred (also called aggression), and Humperdinck is the epitome of greed (also called grasping or passion).

Delusion (or Ignorance): The Vizzini Disease

MAYBE YOU'VE REALIZED BY NOW that it's impossible to know everything. Living in an era when Google is not just a noun but one of our most popular verbs, we see the universe as stocked with facts that each of us does not know, overflowing with phenomena we cannot directly perceive. Every day, we set sail upon a vast ocean of question marks, and we each experience countless opportunities to feel really stupid about all the things we don't know, yet upon which we depend for survival. For example, I consider myself a relatively knowledgeable eater, yet today for lunch I ate a salad containing several ingredients I couldn't recognize. I ingested them anyway, somehow trusting that they wouldn't kill me. How smart is that?

My meditation practice has granted me a fascination with the scope of facts that remain unknown to my mind. I spend a fair amount of time ruminating on the things I may never learn: Thibault's and Capoferro's methods of fencing, how to play the banjo, or what a kiss feels like from my wife's perspective, to name just a few. Thankfully, enlightenment isn't really about *knowing* everything. It's not as if studying Buddhism will make you a great game show contestant. If you want knowledge, you can always use Google, but wisdom doesn't come from search engines.

Knowledge is a very helpful thing. If knowledge leads to greater awareness about how to be kind, or how to create work that benefits people, or how to avoid suffering, then it is immensely useful. But knowledge pales in comparison to the importance of wisdom. Wisdom is much more encompassing; it's an open and clear attitude toward the process of learning itself. Wisdom develops from a curious (rather than presumptuous) attitude toward the process of gaining insight into how reality works. Knowledge is about knowing a thing, but wisdom is about knowing the *nature* of things. Knowledge tells you how something works; wisdom lets you see clearly the larger *context* in which it works, especially the context of impermanence and interdependence. I have often seen one Buddhist word for wisdom, *prajna*, translated by Zen teachers as "before knowing," which refers to the curiosity necessary to discover any truth. Wisdom is what offers you the groundedness to avoid being overwhelmed by any question life may throw at you.

When you don't know the answer to a question, you have only two choices: you can be either curious or defensive. Ignorance is what happens when you take the latter approach. You become insecure, clinging increasingly to whatever you think you know. In Buddhism, ignorance is a more active and destructive form of confusion than just experiencing a moment of not knowing. With ignorance, you literally ignore your own uncertainty, because not knowing the answer is too scary to admit. Ignorance does not come from any lack of knowledge. It comes from the blind assumption of knowledge.

Few characters are a better embodiment of this core

obstacle than the Sicilian Vizzini. Anything that remains outside the reach of Vizzini's assumptions is famously rendered "inconceivable." A modern-day Vizzini would be the person who insists that if it snowed today somewhere on earth, that proves that climate change does not exist. Vizzini has no interest in learning anything new. He is especially not interested in receiving feedback from his hired mercenaries, the friends who, despite all his abuses, are still only trying to help him.

Given the academic and social value we place on the acquisition of information, our culture makes it very difficult for us to feel safe about not knowing facts. We've all had our Vizzini moments. Sometimes our moments of delusion are very subtle. A few years back, a good friend pointed out a little Vizzini tendency of mine. If someone asked me if I'd heard of a musician or artist they were into, I would sometimes blindly say "yeah," even if I wasn't completely sure I knew the artist being mentioned. Maybe I did this to avoid looking like a social outcast, to feel included, up to date. When my friend playfully pointed out that I couldn't possibly have heard all these bands, I realized my habit was an unconscious defense against looking stupid. And, just like most defense mechanisms, it had the opposite of its intended effect. It didn't make me smarter to claim to know something I didn't. Claiming to know wasn't a flat-out lie, which was part of my internal Vizzini justification. I thought I *might* have heard of the artists in question. And yet, my "yeah" answers didn't do anyone any good. Even if I thought I knew whom my friend was talking about, it would've been much wiser to say, "I don't think so. Tell me about them."

That way, even if I heard information I already had, at least there was a chance of expanding my horizons. If I claimed to already know, my friend wouldn't say more, and I would have no chance of learning something new. If I claimed to know, I could only look stupid; yet if I claimed *not* to know, strangely, I could only get smarter.

Vizzini's insecurity about his own knowledge is a bit more aggressive, and the consequences for him are far more severe. Anytime his assertions are threatened, he starts yelling, claiming stupidity or madness on the part of the questioner. He reminds me of many an Internet troll, sans Internet. Fezzik and Inigo could not be gentler in pointing out their boss's confusion, but it's all for naught. Vizzini is every delusional boss who can't empower his employees to succeed, every bad teacher who forgets that a mentor can and should also learn from his students. When you have no curiosity about your uncertainty, you fall victim to your inner Vizzini, and you will always end up swallowing poison.

Vizzini's unwillingness to face uncertainty is exactly what gets him killed.[2] His death happens when he falls headfirst into the clearest conceptual trap of all Buddhist philosophy. In his arrogance, he views the world through the false lens of either/or. He agrees to a game of wits with the Man in Black, but his views can accommodate only two mutually exclusive possibilities. The deadly iocane powder is either in one cup or the other. *How could anything else be possible? I already know everything I need to know. There are only two choices in this world. Black or white. Right or wrong. This cup or that one.* He can't imagine possibilities that exist outside the dualistic frame on which he fixates.

Once the Man in Black locks Vizzini into the either/or, he is able to defeat him by introducing a new possibility lying cleverly outside the binary. *Maybe, just maybe, both cups are poisoned. Maybe I've developed an immunity to the poison we are both about to drink. Did you ever think of that, little Vizzini in my head?* Maybe, instead of shouting, "Inconceivable!" or whispering, "I know that already," we could each get a little more curious, ask a few more questions, and consider a few more possibilities outside the frames we are caught within, before the things we are so sure we know end up causing harm.

A true genius has a very different aura, a kind of thoughtful curiosity, attuned to the topic at hand but free from assumption. Wisdom makes your eyes wide. You ask lots of questions. Have you noticed that during a news interview, the person asking the question is almost always the one who holds the most power in the exchange? A wise person doesn't always tip their hand by telling you their views immediately, unless directly requested to do so.

This curiosity in the face of uncertainty doesn't mean you should pretend *not* to know things you definitely do know. When asked to describe your previous work experience at a job interview, I don't recommend responding with "That's a great question. What *is* my experience?" But if you develop confidence in your own curiosity, then your willingness to not know becomes a sword of clear perception. The only way to realize what you want to say is to start by knowing that you have no idea what you're talking about. The only way to figure out what to do is to realize you have no idea what you're doing. The only way to gain wisdom is to become curious about that recurring question mark. Good friendship is the arena that allows us to develop trust in the uncertainty that lies in the space before knowing. Friends remind us that it's okay not to know everything, and that is how to develop the wisdom to defeat the Vizzini within.

Hatred (or Aggression): The Six-Fingered Man

COUNT RUGEN, THE SIX-FINGERED MAN, has never met a torture device he didn't love. The Count is willing to slaughter a man who spent a year crafting a sword for him, and in front of the man's eleven-year-old son, no less. He will siphon a year from your life using a magical torture apparatus, a contraption that makes waterboarding look like sipping lemonade, and then he will be callous enough to ask how the experience felt, like a waiter asking if you've enjoyed your meal. Count Rugen represents the next of the three core enemies: hatred (or aggression).

This level of intended cruelty, in thought, speech, and action, certainly exists in our world. Where does it come from? In Buddhist terms, hatred comes from an inability to make room for the inevitable experience of anger. Hatred is a hardened resentment toward one's own pain and suffering. Hatred always operates on this skewed logic: *I feel awful, and you should, too.*

Anger only becomes a problem when we don't know how to work with the inherent sadness of not getting what we want. Irritation is an integral part of moment-by-moment experience, and if we don't make room for pain and disappointment, hatred starts to grow. As a habitual pattern, hatred convinces us that the best response to pain is to spread the damage. In extreme karmic cases, like the Count's, hatred becomes so engrained and habitual that it turns pleasurable, which is when hatred becomes cruelty. For most people, our experience of aggression is internally uncomfortable, but for a true bad guy like the Six-Fingered Man, torturing others has become his performance art. When you meditate during times of conflict and resentment, your mind might seem like an internal torture chamber, a space so full of self-aggressive thoughts that you start to take solace in the negativity. You might even miss the hateful thoughts when they disappear for a moment, and then go looking for a new problem so you have something to resent again. When we can't meet anger directly, we over-identify with the object that triggered the emotion, needing to eliminate the perceived source so as not to feel the uncomfortable feeling it brings up.

Sometimes our internal pits of despair turn us into rage-aholics. I often teach meditation during rush hour in Manhattan. As such, the class's mindfulness practice is frequently set against loud background noise: a cacophony of car horns and sirens, a parade of slow-moving commuters who might, possibly, be misdirecting their anger, ever so slightly. When someone chooses to honk their horn while stuck in traffic, more often than not their time in commute is not reduced. A car horn helps you avoid accidents, yes, but it usually doesn't get you home any quicker. I joke that in an enlightened society, car horns would work a bit differently. When someone pressed their horn, a voice would softly declare to everyone on the street, apologetically, "Sooooorrrrrrrry. I'm having a really hard time."

Now, does anyone (other than maybe Count Rugen) excitedly think, as they honk their horn, "I'm about to screw with the sympathetic nervous systems of everyone in a two-block radius!" Probably not. But as we become more habituated to our own cruel thoughts in reaction to discomfort, we begin to lose track of whether those thoughts, and the choices we make when we react to them, actually resolve the pain we're experiencing, or just spread that pain to others. Anger always has something to teach us about sadness, about grief, and about injustice. All these truths need to be addressed. Cruelty, however, attempts a trick that will always backfire: to get rid of a painful feeling that has already happened.

In *The Princess Bride*, Inigo ends up killing the Six-Fingered Man. It's the only time in the movie that a good guy kills a bad guy. Is violent revenge really how a warrior of compassion is meant to defeat the enemy who embodies hatred? Probably not. So is Inigo's fight against Count Rugen too violent to be considered a Buddhist act? Perhaps. Although, to be fair, it does at least stop a villain, a power-mad man addicted to torture, from causing any more harm. After all, there are multiple Buddhist stories of enlightened masters using violence without hesitation to stop a tyrant who couldn't otherwise be stopped. But by the end of *The Princess Bride*, it is also possible that Inigo has recognized that he made a mistake. He does not express regret for his action, but rather the way he chose to view his purpose in life.

Mandy Patinkin was generous enough to speak with me at length about this project, and about the compassionate essay "The Real Politics in *The Princess Bride*," which he wrote for *Time* magazine in response to Sen. Ted Cruz's odd and forceful love of the movie. As Patinkin wrote, "Inigo Montoya spent his life trying to avenge the murder of his father. He found the six-fingered man, and he killed him. But he realized that that did not bring his father back. It didn't do any good. Inigo realized that he might have made a different choice to do something else with his life."[3]

What is it that Inigo decides to do, having spent his life seeking revenge only to be left empty-handed after the deed is done? Possibly, the finale hints, he decides to become the next Dread Pirate Roberts, which, as we will see, is this story's goofy version of a lineage of warriors.[4] Even if we make a mistake, even if hatred gets the better of us, we can always recover, reset, and begin again. Let's hope Inigo made a nonviolent choice for his future.

Patinkin has certainly taken a compassionate approach in his own life. It turns out that he is now a committed meditation practitioner—twenty minutes each day. That's right: Inigo Montoya meditates every day. No pressure, though.

Humperdinck's Greed
(or Passion or Grasping)

PRINCE TRUMPERDINCK . . . ER, HUMPERDINCK IS driven by his hunter's ambition to recapture Buttercup and frame Guilder for her murder so he can take over the rival nation, expanding his domain. His is a classic case of greed, the last of the three core enemies in Buddhist psychology. We can also refer to greed variously as passion, grasping, craving, or even obsession. In Buddhism, greed is a consumptive force, the bloated product of an ancient insecurity. The anxiety that fuels greed comes from fear that the world won't provide you with what you need. Greed comes from an engrained sense of being undernourished or unseen. Within its grasp, you overestimate the resources needed to confirm that you belong, and underestimate the positive qualities you already possess. You go on the hunt, you gobble up physical territory, you even try to consume spiritual accomplishments. For Humperdinck, greed's vanity knows no bounds, because no one is ever paying enough attention to him. He wants Buttercup all to himself. Of course, it could be argued that, just like Rugen, his true emotional hang-up is aggression, because he plans to kill Buttercup on their wedding night in order to start a war with Guilder. What he really wants, though, is more land, which is the fairy-tale version of growing your "brand." From beginning to end, greed is Humperdinck's agenda, and vanity his weakness. At the movie's climax, the mere notion that Westley might be strong enough to disfigure him makes him cower and surrender.

How do you work with the three core enemies of delusion, hatred, and greed? First, you develop a sense of humor, realizing that since before the dawn of civilization and regardless of culture, human beings have been susceptible to these traps, and about eighty-four thousand offshoots of confused beliefs and accompanying behaviors. The next step is to form a sincere aspiration not to further empower the enemies who represent these poisonous traits, either internally or externally.

Meditation and reflection can help you work with these obstacles. A teacher, mentor, or therapist can help you spot these bad guys in your own experience. But it is your close friends, and how you relate to friendship as both a process and a practice, that can give you the support to overcome your enemies. Your best friends are there to practice alongside you as you storm the castle.

Find Your Inner Fezzik

The Practice of Friendship

SINCE THE FOURTH GRADE, I HAVE LEARNED MANY things about being a basically good friend. Have I defeated all my inner villains? Of course not. Am I a great friend to those close to me? I aspire to be one, and now I have much better tools to work with the demons in my own mind. Luckily, we don't live in a world where plots reach their climax after ninety minutes of action. We usually have more time. We have the time we need to slow down and practice.

I have a group of close friends I see regularly for a morning coffee. All of us do creative work for a living (writing, electronic music, painting, sculpture), and all of us meditate. We each take a deep interest in contemporary culture, politics, and society. I often see this group right after completing my morning meditation and yoga. For me, it is crucial to see these comrades on a regular basis, just as important to my work as my early morning wellness practices—even when we are all busy with family or career. Seeing my friends is not the thing I do *after* my practice. Seeing my friends is *part* of my practice.

Given that there is no such thing as a relationship expert, friendship is not something to be mastered. It's a slow, nonlinear parade of interactions with a chosen comrade, a peer who chooses to engage in the process with you. Like any other process, friendship includes loads of discomfort, piles of mistakes, and the need to work with both regret and forgiveness. If Buddhism has anything to say about friendship, or any other type of relationship, it is this: if life is going to lead toward awakening, you have to come to view everything you do, both on and off your meditation cushion, as a *practice*.

Practice Does Not Make Perfect

PRACTICE IS NOT JUST SOME Eastern jargon, although the word often gets dismissed as such. Instead, it's a useful code word for a much bigger shift in perspective on the purpose of life. If you think life is solely about outcomes, about the moments when you achieve long-awaited results, then all I have to say is get used to disappointment.

Outcomes are fleeting, and beyond the credentials or memorabilia they might deliver, their impermanence is often painful. After the achievement fades, a strange thing always happens—a new present moment checks you out, taps you on the shoulder, and whispers a frustrating question in your ear: "So, now what?" Results only lead to new beginnings. Destinations quickly become points of departure. Credits, they roll. The process, the practice, is the only continuity. This flow is perhaps more apparent with friendship than anything else, because in friendship, there is literally no outcome to achieve, except the satisfaction of the process itself.

Buddhism focuses on impermanence, which asks us to pay real attention to the fact that outcomes are unreliable vehicles for the delivery of permanent satisfaction. For this reason, Buddhist thought is sometimes stereotyped as being harshly anti-achievement. This is a misguided interpretation of the dharma. Buddhist thought focuses a surprising portion of its teachings on achieving outcomes, especially when it comes to the more qualitative success that comes with developing traits·like mindfulness, compassion, and wisdom. Some classic Buddhist texts even read like a detailed street map of positive mental and emotional achievements, clearly defining increases in empathy, attention, creative awareness, and one's ability to overcome anxieties about death, to name just a few. Sometimes we achieve profoundly validating outcomes in life, and these triumphs are thoroughly worthy of celebration. If you feel frustration that you have not accomplished something you want, whether it's publication, true love, or saving the world, then I sincerely hope your success is realized and that the results greatly benefit others, too.

The *purpose* of our seeking achievements needs to be contextualized. In the flow of time, achieving a result is just one more moment, one of many. Reality offers no particular privilege to our subjectively defined "big" moments. The space-time continuum does not hold annual award ceremonies. Big moments are a construct. There is nothing wrong with a construct, as long as we don't forget that we built it ourselves. Viewing life as a practice gives you the opportunity to look at experience as a progression, continuous instead of finite, analog rather than digital. A practice involves working to cultivate qualities and attitudes, rather than accumulating trophies bound to tarnish and disintegrate. Our sense of time does not need to be reduced to the anxious buildup to a few anticipated "big" moments, followed by the longer-lived letdown when those moments fade. Mindfulness allows us to see that more moments matter than we previously were willing to acknowledge. Maybe, just maybe, *all* the moments matter.

Practice has not made me perfect. It has only helped me become more aware of my inner villains of delusion, hatred, and greed than I once was, more able to greet them like characters in a beloved movie when they come to visit, rather than bowing down to them as CEOs of consciousness. I've committed many of the classic blunders in friendship over the last thirty years: arrogance, unintended cruelty, dishonesty, and being numb to other people's feelings. And without awareness of my own inner movie, I wouldn't have been able to spot my bad guys, much less work to defeat them. Most of my progress along the path of awakening has been due to friendship, especially treating friendship as a practice every bit as important as sitting on a cushion.

Mindfulness and compassion are skills, not outcomes. There isn't any final exam. You can work with your mind day by day, month by month, and year by year. You don't have to be free from confusion by tomorrow. In fact, meditation masters have said you should only check in with how meditation practice is transforming your life once every ten years, rather than once every ten minutes. The notion of progress without a deadline for perfection is liberating and anxiety-reducing in and of itself.

My teacher Sakyong Mipham likes to point out that we are always practicing something. This means that no matter what you do, you are always cultivating some quality. When you post an obnoxious comment online, you are "practicing" sarcasm. When you check your phone too often, you are "practicing" (dopamine-rewarded) distraction. And when you set an intention and gently gather your mind back into the perceptions of the current moment, you are practicing mindfulness. The choices we make about the activities we participate in reveal our preferences regarding how we want to practice.

Every practice is defined by a specific view and intention. Anytime you take on a practice, you could ask yourself, "Why?" What is the purpose of practicing friendship? If friendship is treated as a practice, it can lead to the gradual disempowerment of your inner obstacles and the emergence of your own wisdom. The purpose of friendship is to help both participants slowly overcome delusion, hatred, and greed.

You don't need to define every practice the same way you define meditation. It's not like you have to ring a gong when you get together with a friend or bow to each other. (Although, what is a hug, handshake, or high five if not our culture's more tactile version of a bow?) The ceremonial aspects of meditation (bows and gongs and candles) serve to remind us of the view, intention, and parameters of a practice. Rituals are everywhere. Friendship has its own ceremonies, even if it is looking someone in the eye during a toast, remembering birthdays, or taking a walk together. The ceremonies of friendship are worth honoring.

For me, the practice of awakened friendship includes the cultivation of three core qualities, and these three qualities are what help transform delusion, hatred, and greed, respectively. These three qualities are trust, inspiration, and generosity.

Trust

THE PRINCESS BRIDE IS ALL about people learning to trust each other. The characters often remind me of my own need for support, and my responsibility to support my friends. The film's plot undercuts machismo and presents characters defined by their vulnerability. It is full of moments when friends must rely on one another during raw exposure to danger, even before their friendship is well established. Inigo and Buttercup must trust Fezzik to pull them up the aptly named Cliffs of Insanity. Westley must trust Inigo to pull him up the same cliffs, even while they're expecting a gentlemen's fight to the death once he reaches the top. Inigo and Fezzik must trust Westley not to kill them when he bests them each in combat. Inigo must trust his best friend, Fezzik, to nurse him back to sobriety so that he can find the Six-Fingered Man, and help Inigo navigate the prince's Zoo of Death[1] and Pit of Despair. Westley must trust Inigo to find him after his torture and help him reincarnate from his "mostly dead" state. Westley must trust them both to help him storm the castle. The movie's heroic climax occurs while the protagonist remains a total invalid—not exactly your *Superman* tale of individual valor. In fact, at least one of the three friends is always incapacitated, vulnerable, or prone to goofy mistakes. Their success occurs through a combination of awkward courage and learning to trust each other.

Trust is how we conquer our inner delusion, or ignorance, our own little Vizzini disease. Delusion arises from an unwillingness to face uncertainty. Overcoming delusion, then, has everything to do with learning to deal with uncertainty. Uncertainty is perhaps the one thing we modern humans are not well equipped to face. It's our evolutionary Achilles' heel. One of my favorite stand-up comedians, John Mulaney, has said, "[When I was a kid] I thought quicksand was going to be a *much bigger* problem than it turned out to be." (Given his age, I can—and will—only presume that this joke was a veiled reference to the infamous Fire Swamp in *The Princess Bride*.)[2] This line is funny because it points to how we are taught, by both evolution and our culture, to fear pretty much everything and everyone we don't already know. We may even fear things that mostly exist in fairy tales and cartoons. From childhood onward, we are taught that if we trust someone, we are probably going to end up drowning. Real quicksand is, thankfully, not one of our main concerns, but fear of embarrassment and rejection are real for all of us, and fear of death is a constant companion.

Evolution alone has not equipped us to deal with uncertainty in a way that is compatible with life in the modern world. According to evolutionary biology, the leftovers of many millennia of predator evasion have given twenty-first-century humans, even those few of us privileged enough to live in relative comfort and safety, a nervous system that biases us to perceive the world and its inhabitants as predatory. Just turn on the news, and you will see very attractive people describing a very ugly world, reminding you to always be shockingly afraid, framing a landscape composed of fire, quicksand, and Rodents of Unusual Sizes, Shapes, and Colors.

On top of these culturally amplified fears lies the vulnerability of our entire human circumstance: that fragile metronome called a heartbeat in your rib cage, those wisps of breath in your lungs keeping you precariously nourished by O_2, that finely tuned proprioception of the inner ear that keeps you from colliding with other bodies in motion. If anything goes wrong with any of these systems, danger ensues. And then there are the universal quicksands of every human life: the inevitable pains of sickness, aging, and death. On top of all this, the entire planet on which all these types of "quicksand" dwell is hurtling through the vast domain of unknowable space. Even if there is no real quicksand in our adult lives, there are a million ways to fear uncertainty.

Then there's relational uncertainty. You never know what other people think of you. When I wonder how someone regards me, I really have only three types of thought. The first is positive certainty: "They like me, they really, really like me." That type of thought is the rarest, in my personal experience. The second type of thought is negative certainty: "They know I'm a loser." Historically, that thought happens more often. The third type of thought, and clearly the most accurate perception, is the thought of true uncertainty: "I have *no idea* what that person thinks of me." Surprisingly, it seems, we are primed to take more comfort (or at least find more familiarity) in assuming the second thought, the loser thought, than allowing for the third thought, true uncertainty. Consider that for a moment. We would rather assume negativity than spend any time contemplating uncertainty! This is a very strange choice, in terms both of accurate thinking and of happiness, but it is a choice that is bred into our evolutionary makeup.

Sometimes I describe the Buddhist path in simple and modern terms. Perhaps Buddhism is just a series of tools for dealing with uncertainty. Maybe mindfulness is the next evolutionary adaptation for modern humans and our maladaptive nervous systems. Perhaps we will all be better off if we learn to hang out, moment by moment, with uncertainty. Trust, and the friendships that allow trust to grow, make us better able to do this difficult work. In a social environment of trust, we can begin to embrace uncertainty as an enriching experience.

Facing existential uncertainty alone is a lot to ask of any individual. Trust involves the belief that another human can remind you of your own basic goodness whenever you don't know what will happen next. Sometimes, my confidence in my own basic goodness gets quite low, like a phone battery in the red zone. Luckily, the Shambhala tradition offers teachings and short meditation practices on how to recharge your courage, in order to plug back into your inner confidence.[3] However, these personal teachings become even more powerful when you can also receive the stored energy of a trusted friend. In friendship, trust is like saying to another person, "I forgot my charger. You mind if I borrow yours?"

If another person can be trusted, they can also become a reliable source of feedback about your life and path. A trusted friend may annoy you from time to time, and they will certainly let you down, but they will also be willing to give you their honest take. Therefore, you can begin to look to them for advice about how your path is going, especially regarding your own inner villains. Of course, we can, and should, also look to teachers or mentors for this kind of feedback, but we see our friends more often than we see anyone else. No matter what kind of guidance we seek, friends usually know us better. Within a trusting friendship, there is a sense of mirrored accountability with another person.

"I got your back" is a very helpful thing to hear when you are trying to build your ability to know your own mind. Good feedback becomes especially crucial in tough moments. The deepest insights usually come from moments of painful vulnerability.

A trusting friendship transforms the meaning of a mistake. In friendships, mistakes come in many shapes and sizes: you tell a joke that lands badly and hurts feelings; you forget to invite somebody, and they feel left out; you forget to acknowledge an act of generosity; you make dishonest excuses for failing to show up; you cave to jealousies you didn't think you still had; you simply let each other down. I've had many friendships that worked well when times were good. But in the best friendships, mistakes are not deemed deal breakers, but rather chances for feedback.

There are only two views of what a mistake is. In a worldview based on the premise that you are sinful and basically bad, mistakes become grounds for shaming. In this distrusting world, a mistake provides further evidence of your dysfunctional nature, verifying that foundational screwup you can't even recall. In a distrusting friendship, mistakes are apocalypses, always the last straw. Or else, a mistake provokes defensiveness, an unwillingness to accept any feedback, and the two friends stop talking to each other about what might not be working. Defensiveness is what happens when shame obstructs vulnerability. Shame acts like a kind of blockade against mindfulness and reflection. When a mistake makes you feel ashamed, you don't even want to look at it. Without being able to put mistakes in the context necessary for reflection, you will never use them to wake up. Awakening requires us to process our mishaps like compost.

When two friends have some level of trust in each other's basic goodness, a mistake becomes something reasonable, neither an atrocity nor something to be shrugged off under some "it's all good" pretense. A trusting friendship puts mistakes in context, illuminating what you need to work on in a way that makes you feel inspired to do that work.

Feedback is a fascinating part of any human relationship. We undoubtedly live in the era when unwelcome feedback is given more often than ever before in human history. Just go online, and you will see people zinging unsolicited opinions at each other constantly, cruel rejoinders that help no one. So often, we turn into Vizzini online, telling everybody else what we know about them. Even if an online comment is accurate, very rarely is the feedback received, much less utilized. Why? Because feedback is almost never useful unless you trust its source. If you don't trust the "friend" giving you feedback, you usually don't hear what they are saying, period. And if you do hear it, it hits your ears as a crushing blow, and shame blocks your ability to incorporate what's been said. In either case, you can't do anything with the feedback.

In my time working closely with students of Buddhism and meditation, I have come to feel that it is useless to offer someone feedback on their actions or beliefs before a trusting relationship has been established. The catharsis of a tell-it-like-it-is moment before a trusting friendship is built is a very short-lived feeling. But when two friends trust each other, something shifts, and they can give each other feedback on their beliefs, actions, and work in the world, opinions that are more useful than almost any other form of feedback. When friends trust each other they ask for advice. When a friend you trust points to a mistake you've made and says, "Why don't you just call and apologize?" it doesn't feel like a red mark against your soul, even though the illumination of a mistake always stings a bit.

In the work I do, I both receive and give a tremendous amount of feedback. I actually hear Inigo's voice when it is time to listen or time to tell it like it is. Like a good friend, Inigo tries to give Vizzini some gentle feedback in one of the most famous lines of the movie: "You keep using that word. I do not think it means what you think it means." There is something in Mandy Patinkin's soft yet perceptive voice, I believe, that has immortalized this line in a movie full of famous lines.[4] I often contemplate this statement, and especially Inigo's voice when uttering it, whenever I think someone is way off in their self-assessment, or has no idea what they're talking about, or gets all their information from the "wrong" media source. Sometimes I hear Inigo's voice in my mind when I realize that, in fact, *I* probably have no idea what I'm doing or saying. In that moment on-screen, Inigo's tone of voice is set to the perfect frequency for awakened feedback.

Inigo is even able to practice what Buddhists call "right speech," assuming responsibility for his own subjectivity: "I do not think it means what you think it means." This is compassionate speech, when what he might really want to say at this point is "On the soul of my father, Domingo

Montoya, you're a moron, Vizzini." A trusting friend doesn't have to say that, because in a trusting friendship, the subtext is obvious. How many times, if I am humble, has a friend tried to tell me that I was confused, and I couldn't hear them just because I didn't want to open myself to the vulnerability of having been wrong? In a good friendship, feedback on your mistakes feels like a surgeon carrying a timely scalpel and a pain reliever. In a harmful friendship, it's like a blackout drunk wielding a sledgehammer. And sometimes, in a deceptively harmful friendship, there's simply no feedback at all.

One of my greatest fascinations is being a fly on the wall and watching people talk to each other. It's amazing to witness the difference between people's communication when they trust each other and how they speak when they don't. You can see it in body language, tone of voice, and willingness to be direct. You can spot a great friendship by how the friends give each other feedback on their mistakes. I have had a few friendships where mistakes became deal breakers. Despite the people involved liking each other tremendously, in the end these friendships weren't beneficial. When a mistake is treated like the end of the road for a relationship, it probably means the relationship wasn't going to help you awaken.

In a friendship based on trust, one person can say to the other something like "You never called me back." Instead of fencing your way into defensive excuses, saying, "Yeah, but I was *so* busy," or "I totally missed your message," you could just say, "Sorry, I messed up." If you can't be vulnerable and trust the basically good intentions of your friend, you can't use this as a teachable moment. If you want that friendship to help you wake up, you might need to spend more time establishing trust as the path to meaningful feedback. Receiving feedback is the only way to avoid the delusion of thinking you already know it all.

Inspiration

MY POSTMEDITATION COFFEE SESSIONS WITH friends are inspiring. Seeing one another allows us to prime the pump of our collective energy, even if we don't discuss the creative work we are each currently doing. Our conversations are caffeine fueled and passionate. We don't just talk about Buddhism, although that topic may come up. We discuss the crazy politics of the day, the newest art opening, or the latest music we've heard. Or else we wax philosophical about how to be a spiritual person in this age of capitalism on steroids without becoming monsters. I leave our meetings feeling inspired to create, inspired to work with others. The inspiration to be creative, curious, and inclusive of ideas is what conquers hatred.

There is nothing wrong with anger. Anger is an extremely creative emotion, because it can help identify and remove obstacles to progress. Anger informs you, often quite vividly, that something is misaligned, or that some injustice exists and must be addressed. But when anger isn't treated carefully, its energy gets caught up in both mind and body. When anger gets stuck, it's as if your nervous system is choosing to run itself on coal power, a pollutive and stressful energy. Hatred is the enemy of creativity, the torturer of inspiration. When we speak of either hatred or aggression, we are referring to the stuck, unaware form of anger.

Hatred leads to a kind of mindless rejection. You flail, trying to dismiss an experience that is already happening. That's why aggression is so uncomfortable internally, because part of you already knows that you're attempting the impossible. That discomfort, and the potential for it to spread like a virus, is why hatred is so destructive.

Classic Buddhism points to the way in which hatred halts the functioning of your intelligence because it impairs your perception of specific phenomena. Intelligence is based on the ability to perceive specificity, the ability to see what causes are bringing about a particular situation. When caught up in hatred, you stop discerning moments for their unique qualities. Proper nouns become pronouns and individuals become vague groups. The situation becomes a vague *that*. Your diagnosis of the problem at hand is increasingly foggy. You say things like "You *always* leave that there," or "(Wo)men suck!" or even "Immigrants need to leave." But none of these issues (the stuckness, the overgeneralization, the violence) is implicit in the human experience of anger. It is only when you perceive an experience directly, without overgeneralizing, that the intelligence of anger gets activated. It is one thing to stub your toe and think, "This is painful right now," and another to think, "Everything *sucks!*" Anger's intelligence makes you want to know what is happening to cause *this* pain right now, how the pain might be avoided or stopped. When anger gets precise, that's when its wisdom is unleashed.

Aided by the mirroring support of a good friendship, inspiration allows room for anger to be just what it is, a passionate truth that wants to find its expression somehow, that longs to change the world for the better. Inspiration provides you an opportunity to do something helpful about what makes you angry. When my coffee posse discussed the 2016 presidential election, for example, we were all quite angry, shocked, and even nauseous. When we could turn that anger, and the sadness lying beneath it, into a creative passion, rather than just passing around more cyclical suffering, we left each meeting inspired to express something helpful, maybe even to volunteer our time for others, rather than drowning in tortured resentments. When you realize that you cannot exclude an experience that is already occurring, you end up inspired to incorporate the painful experience into acts of transformation.

Inspiration is the second practice of a basically good friendship. Friendships help us overcome the Six-Fingered Man who lives inside. Friends feed off of each other's quest for truth. When you are inspired, your shared intention is to create rather than to destroy, to illuminate reality instead of infecting others with more darkness and pain. Inspiration keeps you on fire with insight, rather than being caught up in divisive generalizations.

Inspiration leads to the strengthening of a core aspiration that will only make you happier: to help other people. Declaring an intention for your life is the ultimate way to help others. To set intentions, you need to make time to gain inspiration from your friends. One morning, after coffee with my friends, I felt a wide smile cross my face as I headed off to work. Even in the midst of the world's chaos, I felt ready to go. I heard Christopher Guest's voice saying something the Six-Fingered Man never said, but that perhaps Chris might: "I've just *added* one day to your life. And remember, this is for posterity, so be honest. How do you *feel*?"

Generosity

WHEN WE WERE NO LONGER roommates, that same R.O.U.S.–trapping friend and I used to meet up for meals on a regular basis. Neither of us had much disposable income; we were still struggling through the various cash-flow dilemmas of being twentysomethings. But whenever the bill came, we would both lunge for it. Because we trusted each other, neither of us was mentally tracking who had paid the last time, or whose turn it was now. We were also unwilling to tediously count what each of us owed and split the bill. We would each try to pay the whole thing, every time. It became a game. Whoever grabbed the check got one huge reward that probably isn't very Buddhist: the right to taunt the other. The winner, the one who paid the bill, would get to laugh at the protesting loser, standing up and shouting, "Can you just accept kindness? Why can't you *accept kindness*? Can you???!!!"

Letting go is a powerful expression of the practice of generosity. In our world, generosity is often reduced to calculated and budgeted acts of charity. There's nothing wrong with charity, or with keeping a budget. Charity is better than greed, and a budget is an act of accountability.

But charity often involves making a gift from a place of comfort, walled and bordered within a spreadsheet. In this kind of gift-giving, there is no real challenge to a rigid sense of identity. In fact, we often use charity to *reinforce* identity, waiting for everyone to acknowledge us, expecting events or new wings of buildings to carry our name.

Fezzik is one of the most truly generous characters in all of narrative history, which is why his example should always be obeyed. He is the exact opposite of Humperdinck. *You need me to carry you up that cliff? Sure! All three of you? Okay! You need me to fight the Man in Black for you? Done. You need me to help you get sober, Inigo? Why not? You need me to smash that door in for you? What are friends for? You need me to bring you four white horses at the perfect moment so we can make our escape together? Here you go, lady.* Fezzik embodies the ideal of generosity because there's absolutely nothing in it for him. He's a character without an agenda, which also means he's a character free of greed. His parents gone, he pursues nothing but friendship. Perhaps this makes his character development unrealistic. After all, everyone has ambition, right? Maybe the traumas of his early life, combined with his superhuman strength, make it easier for him to let go of his own needs because he knows he has nothing to prove. It is always easy to let go when you have both great strength and nothing to lose. Maybe Fezzik is just not holding on so tightly to himself.

The confused mind is always holding on to something: an object, an itinerary, an identity. One way to examine the confusion that comes from a rigid sense of self is via the study of psychological concepts such as "ego construction."

But another way to understand the problem of ego is through felt experience: the confused mind simply *feels* tight, like a knotted muscle. In meditation, you often encounter this tightness physically, as bodily tension. You may be gripped by a series of thoughts about what you "need" to happen, thoughts that dissolve when they aren't immediately acted upon. The tightened sense of self creates anxiety at the deepest levels of consciousness. Therefore, the Buddhist practice of generosity is not just about the moral or social implications of charity. Generosity is a mental yoga, an exercise meant to stretch and relax the arthritic rigidity of "me." I imagine my own moments of self-absorption as a tightly closed fist, unable to open. The practice of generosity is the embodied *feeling* of opening that fist, which only happens when the muscles relax. True generosity is not ideological, but muscular. Through ritualized acts of offering, you can practice generosity regularly, and when you do, the mind begins to soften and release. When generosity is fully realized, your identity literally *feels* looser. That's how you know that the practice is working. The verification that an act of generosity was successful has little do with receiving applause; it has to do with a feeling of release.

Letting go in this way is not an easy practice, because relaxing is perhaps the trickiest of all muscular actions, for both body and mind. It is most helpful to first practice letting go with a trusted friend. In the best friendships, you can even create playful games like the game my friend and I play when fighting over the check. There's a good reason to start practicing generosity with close friends first. For one thing, you really can't help *all* sentient beings summit the Cliffs of Insanity. But we should each have a few trusted friends to whom, when they ask you for something, you answer "yes." And not just because your friends need you, but because by offering something spontaneously and unexpectedly, you get to let go of a very small plot of land called "me." That release is what liberation feels like.

The outcome of this release is an increased ability to both give and receive, so practicing generosity usually makes the giver better off than they were before. The more generous you become, the more connections you develop, and the more you end up receiving in return. Once you start to open the fist, things flow in both directions.

Eventually, perhaps, you can let go this way with strangers. Perhaps we could even build whole economies based on generosity and consider an IRS agent to be a trusted friend. But when practicing with a stranger, you aren't sure if the offering will be acknowledged, received, or even understood. The best place to practice generosity is with someone you know also wants to practice it with you.

For many of us interested in meditation, generosity might feel like something we already do too much of. Many meditators work in service to others, and they view meditation practice as a relief from the burden of other people, a crucial form of self-care. Maybe you feel you spend too much of your professional or personal life taking care of people. Maybe, just like Andre the Giant, the burden of being Fezzik in your own life has given you serious back problems.[5] Sometimes it feels like we need to be more selfish. Maybe empathy is overrated. Maybe those of us who work with others would feel better if we conjured more greed.

I understand this impulse, but greed doesn't help. When I have felt this way, I've realized that I still need to employ the same principle of generosity, and even more diligently, just directed inward. If I am overtaxed and spent from offering myself to others, it doesn't mean generosity is obsolete. When properly practiced, generosity always leads to a feeling of release and liberation. If I feel burnt out, all it means is that I need to practice offering to myself, with the exact same ceremonial *feeling* of opening and letting go as I would to a trusted friend. Sometimes, in order to feel worthy of the gift of my own generosity, I need to regard myself in the third person. I find myself saying things like "Ethan is a basically good guy, right? He looks like he needs a break. Let's get Ethan a pillow." Offering is a ritual that never steers you wrong, whether the recipient is yourself or others. Greed is a ceremony of narcissism that never rewards anyone. Rather than waiting for someone else to make the first move, the most liberating approach is to become the first person to let go of your itinerary. OBEY Fezzik by becoming Fezzik.

Every Relationship Starts with the Practice of Friendship

I AM ALWAYS FASCINATED that one of the main Buddhist words for "teacher," *mitra*, literally translates as "friend." While being a Buddhist teacher is not the same as being somebody's close friend—we do not generally help students move their couches—it is a mutual relationship, a relationship that exists to help both people conquer their inner bad guys. Insofar as the student-teacher connection is a form of friendship, it is also a relationship based on trust, inspiration, and generosity on both sides. Trust allows you to live together in a groundless world and conquer the delusion of certainty. Inspiration allows you to live creatively, defeating the hatred that comes from rejecting your own pain. Generosity allows you to let go of grasping and to inhabit a much larger world, a world that includes far more than "me."

The world has seen few close friendships as long-lasting as my father's lifelong journey with the man who pretended to be the embodiment of cruelty in *The Princess Bride*. For sixty-nine years and counting, Christopher and David have helped each other conquer many bad guys, mostly internal, and perhaps a few bad guys "out there," the various bullies on life's many playgrounds. Sometimes closer, sometimes farther apart, each has let the other be himself.

A great friendship is one of the most admirable of all spiritual experiences because it helps you see basic goodness when you look in the mirror. I may never be blessed by a friendship with quite the longevity of Chris and David's, but I aspire to that sort of longevity in my own practice of befriending myself, and in my practice with my current friends. Seeing friendship as a practice has been every bit as important as working with my own mind on the meditation cushion. If you find good companions to practice with, no bad guy will stand a chance. The support of friendship might prepare you for the difficult journey of intimate relationships. It might even begin to open the doorway to true love.

PART II

THE DHARMA OF ROMANCE

Aaaaaaaaaas . . . youuuuuuuuuu . . .
wiiiiiiiiisssshhhhh.

—THE SOUND OF DEVOTION ROLLING PAINFULLY
DOWN A VERY BUMPY, VERY STEEP HILL

There Is No Buttercup

Every love story is a ghost story.

—DAVID FOSTER WALLACE

WE ALL HAVE TO SAY GOODBYE TO BUTTERCUP. AT
least, we have to let go of the false salvation embedded
in the myth that there is one. I said goodbye to the woman
I thought was my Buttercup when I was just about to turn
thirty, in the spring of 2008. We didn't part ways on a bucolic green in Florin, like Westley and his love. Instead,
it was a quiet but sad spring evening in New York City's

"bucolic" Tompkins Square Park. I began the evening deeply afraid of how damaged our connection had grown since we moved in together almost a year before. I felt as if I were clutching a child's clumsy art project made of papier-mâché, a project whose structural integrity was coming undone before my eyes, on the way to being graded by the proverbial teacher.

What had been falling apart for a year was now about to dissolve completely; we just were not going to work out as a couple. If we wanted to hunt for blame, there were lots of possible causes: my busy schedule and the stress of starting a nonprofit organization while publishing my first book, which led to inattention; or her panic attacks, which had become intense, invasive, and nightly; or our growing inability to communicate in any way in which we each felt heard and understood by the other. On this particular evening, we circled the park again and again, discussing what we wanted out of life, what we each wanted for ourselves, what we had both wanted together a year ago, and whether those desires were compatible now. By the end of the evening, I knew that we lived in misaligned universes. In difficult times, we didn't communicate with each other in anything close to sustainable ways. I was also realizing, perhaps selfishly, that I didn't want the duty of caretaking all at once a new organization, students, and a partner struggling with clinical anxiety. After a period together that had begun torridly and idyllically before twisting into a nightmare, it was time for me to let go of "us," to set out on the high seas of single life once again. I felt the ambivalence that accompanies the end of an unworkable commitment.

Loneliness came in waves, but I also felt the excitement of freedom's onset. A few weeks later, when my olfactory memory was overwhelmed by smelling shampoo that reminded me of her, I was revisited by an old thought, a thought I'd always found both profound and profoundly unsettling: freedom and loneliness come from the same place.

The Farmboy's story, of course, is different from mine, far more fairy tale. Westley gets to return to the same Buttercup he left behind years earlier. Wouldn't it be fantastic if, after all our spiritual and psychological transformations out there on the high seas, we each got to return to our O.G. Buttercups, our first loves, our most seminal romances? Not many of us have such luxury. Whether we learn from experience or not, most of the time we simply have to move on and get ready for the next connection, a new now.

The Farmboy realizes his true love for Buttercup, and she eventually returns his epiphany, but he is too poor to marry her. So he sets out across the sea to find the resources necessary to earn the fortune he'll need so they can begin their life together.[1] Like the Farmboy, I realized on that night in 2008 that I had found someone "spiritual," someone smart, someone creative, someone beautiful, but not someone with whom I could communicate genuinely and deeply during confusing or hard times. Without that huge missing piece, I didn't have the resources for a partnership. Just like the Farmboy, I was sentenced by my karma to exactly five more years adrift on the rocky seas of modern dating before finding my partner. To find her, I had to leave my romantic idols behind, and renounce my membership in the Church of Soul Mates.

Overcoming the Theism of Romance

THE PRINCESS BRIDE UNDERMINES THE cheesy ideals of classic fairy tales while still fully celebrating true love. Mindfulness, as both cognitive technique and more general worldview, is about relinquishing ideals and embracing the felt truth of the present moment. Buddhism, as a paradigm, is about awakening the compassion and awareness that naturally arise *after* the deconstruction of false views. This all sounds quite nice in theory. But in practice, repeatedly seeing your ideals collapse and finding the strength to return again and again to the way things are, not the way you want them to be, is usually a painful challenge. This challenge is exacerbated by life in an era when momentarily escaping from the present moment is becoming exponentially easier. When we remember all the difficult feelings involved in sex, romance, communication, and partnership—well, let's just say it makes sense that many practitioners throughout history have chosen the path of celibacy.

In creating *The Princess Bride*, the author and screenwriter William Goldman seemed intent, every step of the way, on poking fun at the standards that classic fairy tales offer up. Goldman works with humor by deconstructing archetypes. Each of his characters deviates hilariously from fairy-tale norms, which is what makes them each so memorable. His evil geniuses are not very smart at all, his master swordsmen are also sloppy drunks, his giants are tender poets, and his unbeatable pirate warrior becomes crippled with despair and only gets by with a lot of help from his friends. Even Goldman's miracle-producing wizard is dejected and insecure about his own wizardry, like a clinically depressed Gandalf!

Humor is the most loving method of deconstruction, and it is essential for any spiritual path. Chögyam Trungpa used to refer to the attempt to find solidity within our existence as a "cosmic joke," a sort of irresolvable dilemma that, once we give up trying to solve it, could potentially open us up to both wonder and appreciation. When we try to hold reality together under a unifying and inflexible belief system, we usually end up taking everything way too seriously. Laughter is the physical response to seriousness cracking under its own pressure. As one of his central instructions for enlightenment, an ancient Tibetan master named Longchenpa had this to say:

> *Since everything is but an apparition,*
> *Perfect in being what it is,*
> *Having nothing to do with good and bad, acceptance*
> * or rejection,*
> *You might as well burst out laughing!*

Most important, William Goldman brings his comedic deconstruction of a fairy tale into the realm of romance. His immaculate beauty, the model object of all heterosexual male fantasies, the title character in *The Princess Bride* is named . . . Buttercup.

I still remember the moment, at age nine, when I first heard the name Buttercup. *That's a really weird name for a girl*, I thought. Why would William Goldman name the most idealized object of sexual affection in his piece something so ridiculous? Because he understands, and we also understand, at least intellectually, that our romantic ideals are often that ridiculous. Clinging to our ideals usually takes us away from, not toward, happiness.

Let's be honest: on its surface, *The Princess Bride* is a story with some very sexist elements. The characters reinforce the gendered narrative of a patriarchal society: the intelligent yet powerless damsel-in-distress who must be rescued from her captor by her male love interest and his very male friends.[2] Yet the story also attempts to undercut such stereotypes. Obviously it's impossible to uncouple gender from power in our society, but to the extent that they can be distinguished, the spiritual significance of Buttercup is not so much about gender. It's about the objectification of romance. It's about walking the fine line between admiration and idealization, finding that razor's edge between true love and rom-coms.

From this perspective, Buttercup is a commentary on objectification, and a calling-out of the rom-com myth. Her name doesn't need to represent a woman (despite Robin Wright's feminine . . . um, radiance in the role). Your ideal prince or princess could identify as female, male, or without gender. If you are attracted to men, you could just as easily call this impossible archetype "Prince Studmuffin." The Buttercup myth (which could be called less humorously the soul mate myth) embodied in most contemporary rom-com scripts is about a trap of belief that's hard to recognize and even harder to escape. At one time or another, you fall victim to the myth that the perfect person might just come

along and save you. Save you from what? What do you need
to be saved from? The only thing any human being has ever
really wanted to be saved from: dealing with your own mind.

In Buddhism, we emphasize the danger of fixating upon
saviors. Chögyam Trungpa called Buddhism a "nontheis-
tic" tradition. *Nontheism* was a conscious word choice on his
part, and is not the same thing as atheism (as in the concrete, perhaps arrogant statement "I am certain that there
is no god"). When Chögyam Trungpa illuminated his use
of the word *nontheism*, he did not discard the idea of sacredness or divinity, which is crucial to awakening, at least in
the Tantric Buddhist tradition he practiced and taught.
There are many definitions of god and divinity that do not
propose an external savior, a conscious actor separate from
the creation they established. I am convinced that when my
more religious friends speak of God, they are talking of
the inherent sacredness of this world, not some dude sitting
on a cloud who can solve our problems for us. This vision of
divinity as an inherent sacredness is entirely in line with
Buddhist thought.

Nontheism refers to something more psychological,
something more practical. When he spoke of "theism,"
Chögyam Trungpa was calling our attention to the way we
look for external saviors to take ourselves away from the
tedious, uncomfortable, and lonely work of being with ourselves. For him, this painful grasping after idols was a
distancing mistake, the tragedy of many forms of worship.
Pursuing these escapist detours, which he also called spiritual materialism, can take on many different relational and
cultural forms.

Blind faith in a separate creator god is one classic form of theism. However, in the twenty-first century, we need to pay attention to a wider collection of theistic traps. When wanting false salvation from your own mind, or wanting to numb yourself from the awkwardness and fears inherent in participating in human relationships, you might invest in a whole array of false prophets. Most of our false prophets are now found outside of churches or temples. Many of our most popular forms of salvation would now be categorized as secular, not religious.

Clarifying this subtle and more personal definition of theism becomes more important now, especially for the growing number of us who don't subscribe to any belief in an omnipotent creator, who don't want to identify with any traditionally regarded "spiritual" group. We live in an age when fewer people believe in a creator god than ever, with more agnostics and atheists than ever before.[3] However, this does not exempt any of us from the trap of theism. An atheist can be just another kind of believer, worshipping false cures, taking solace in beliefs that simply cannot be proven in experience, all the while escaping from their own heart and mind. Buddhists often fall into the trap of theism as well. Even though there is no creator god in classic Buddhism, a Buddhist who believes they might be saved by finding the right guru's blessing, or the right meditation technique, or the right material for the beads in their mala bracelet, is just another kind of theist. This tragic idea that there is some way to avoid dealing with who you are forms the basis for all theistic confusion, whether that confusion turns you into a religious fundamentalist or a shopaholic. Whatever your poison, theism involves the tragic externalization of your own worthiness as a human.

Theistic confusion doesn't just happen once. It recurs, moment by moment, and while you're on your path, your quest for a savior can take many different forms. Because it is one of the most valued cultural centers in modern society, our chosen temple of worship might be a movie theater. More specifically, there's the myth embedded in the romantic comedy, the wish that the right partner might grant you the right status, saving you from a lonely life struggling against your own mind. Many of us worship Prince Studmuffin or Princess Buttercup, even if we call them by less satirical names. Most of us would never admit that we are seeking a Buttercup, of course. *Are you kidding? Not me.* The worst kind of fairy tale is a fantasy that can't admit it is one. Most rom-coms are modern fairy tales that don't admit they're peddling fantasies. *The Princess Bride* is a great reminder of the need for humor in the age of romantic theism, the era of Buttercups and Studmuffins who don't exist.

Whatever your gender identity or sexual orientation, let's try this. You and I are the Farmboy, the Farmgirl, or the Farmkid. The Farmkid must train as a pirate warrior of love in a harsh world, seeking middle ground in a culture driven by extreme beliefs about romance on all sides: blind soul mate seekers on your right and bitter cynics on your left. Buttercup represents that perpetual and idealized "other," whatever romantic object you chase. Even if you aren't seeking a life partner, you still might chase the "other" anytime desire takes hold of your body and mind. If you are human, desire is inescapable.

Labeling the "other" as Buttercup is compelling because we can name this myth in our own minds, and then laugh at ourselves a bit, without losing faith in love. If we are going to awaken, we must recover our sense of humor. We also can't lose sight of love's ability to guide us toward genuine admiration and an integration of the positive qualities we find in other humans. The road you learn to walk, the journey of true love, is the middle path. The "Middle Way" is an ancient Buddhist philosophical system that calls awareness to a general tendency of the confused mind.[4] We tend to careen back and forth between extreme approaches, neither of which leads us to satisfaction. Walking the middle path doesn't mean you never stumble or get lost. All it requires is that you become a curious student of your own extreme beliefs and slowly learn how not to get caught in either pole. When it comes to romance, the two extremes I have spotted again and again are (1) belief in salvation and (2) cynicism about the whole damn thing. On the middle path of romance, you will need to bring your heart along with you. It's even okay to be a bleeding-heart, love-stricken Buddhist romantic just like me. In fact, you might find it to be essential.

The Buttercup Checklist

IN MY EARLY TWENTIES, AS we entered the new millennium, I was somewhere around my twelfth or fourteenth viewing of the movie. In my postcollegiate years, I was also carrying a checklist around in the back pocket of my mind. I don't know if you've ever made a list of the qualities your ideal partner would have. I know some people who have kept actual lists, clearly documented and crisply bullet-pointed, out of deep hopefulness of finding a partner; or, more humbly, a list hewn together out of deep frustration at missing meaningful signs the last time they opened their hearts to someone. Most often, our ideal lists are crafted from a blend of past frustration and hopefulness for the future. I know of a few people who, after disappointments overwhelmed them, literally set their lists on fire, a ceremonial catharsis that was one part Wiccan ritual, one part quasi-Buddhist purification of karma, one part made-up New Age spiritual mumbo-jumbo.

Whether we formally bullet-point the qualities we seek in another person or merely keep them at the back of our minds, we each track what we're looking for, chasing admirable qualities loosely defined somewhere in the realm of anxious thoughts and urgent impulses. Of course, you might keep multiple lists for different life situations, lists of expectations that may have little or no overlap with one another: the One-Night Stand list, the Casual Commitment list, the Father of My Child list, the Person I Want to Grow Old With list, and the Screw It, Let's Be Self-Destructive Again Tonight list. We all make notes about our perceived needs as we check people out, scouring the human terrain, or the virtual terrain of some app, like a Terminator scanning for its target. On top of the stress of maintaining internal checklists, there are the outcomes our friends and family want for us, outcomes imposed or amplified by culture, social networks, and peer pressure. Friends tell you (after you've already gotten hurt) to watch for the "red flags" that *they* saw so clearly, those signs that, if only you'd been thinking straight, would have let you know that the person you wanted was a zero instead of a hero, a situation too problematic to be anything other than a step in the wrong direction.

In my early twenties I had a list going, a list of those qualities that might constitute my Buttercup. You would never get me to admit such a list existed, not even to myself. Some people keep a journal, but that wasn't my style. Our views and beliefs are not always so explicit as to be written down somewhere. Most of the time, our actions inferentially reveal to us the views that dominate our consciousness. Our views lay the groundwork for our actions, but our actions reveal our views after the fact. The Buttercup list was there, qualifications and qualities wallpapering my skull, rib cage, and groin.

It may seem somehow superficial, or "un-Buddhist," to name qualities of romantic expectation, but if you've made it this far into the book, let's agree to let someone else be the Superficiality Police, okay? I've grown weary of prefabricated judgments about which thoughts are profound and which are superficial, judgments rendered all too easily, carelessly indicting the full spectrum of *actual* feelings that a human being might *actually* experience while *actually* being human. If you are curious about life, if you practice mindfulness and compassion, you are going to come across some superficial thoughts and views, both in your own mind and in the minds of other basically good humans.

Some superficial beliefs come from privilege, some come from prejudice, some come from fear and trauma, and all come from karma. Without the ability to become lovingly aware of superficial or prejudiced beliefs, or if you are immediately ashamed at their existence, you can't work with your *actual* thoughts. When it comes to romantic attraction and aversion, if you aren't curious about your turn-ons and turn-offs, then the illumination offered by mindfulness is rendered inoperative before it can begin.

The truth is, superficial qualities can lead to depth in time, because superficial thoughts can lend insight about what we admire in another person. The word *superficial* simply refers to a surface, and every object has a surface, even those objects called thoughts. The surface is never a problem, because the façade is simply a doorway to a deeper experience. When two people meet, they first examine each other superficially. But appearances can be misleading when there's nothing underneath, and the bubble of artifice pops, leaving you lost, without deeper intent or values to guide you. Too often, I've noticed, meditators are only looking for profundity. But reality has many surfaces. We have a tendency to shame our superficial thoughts before they've even been observed and appreciated for what they are. Without appreciating your own superficiality, you won't ever arrive at profundity.

In my early twenties, having that abstract list of ideals—most of them hollow and fantasy-driven, a few with depth and grounded in a connection with others—was all quite timely. Five or so years into a meditation practice that became consistent at the end of high school, I was finally discerning what kind of person I wanted to be, at least for the time being—according to modern neuroscience, my male brain was just completing its adult formation. I was also trying to figure out how a person could pay their rent in this world without feeling like a mostly dead sell-out. I was practicing Buddhism and meditation seriously, and decided that, in some way, I wanted to teach those things (though I had no idea until later that it might become a career). I was also trying to be a creative and, as much as possible, politically conscious person. These decisions felt important, perhaps (like everything else in your twenties) a little too important. I was also trying to figure out dating, a quest that felt like a blindfolded scavenger hunt through a junkyard of random advice. Opinions on dating were readily offered up by pretty much everyone I knew, generated in every medium of communication the early twenty-first century could offer, and at every social forum. An assembly of voices claimed impossible expertise in locating Buttercups and Studmuffins for others, as if perfect mates were falling from trees.

My past lent me little help in figuring out romance. I had a lot of great guidance in many other aspects of my spiritual path—but dating? To be honest, both my familial and spiritual heritages offered much general wisdom regarding life, the universe, and everything, but almost nothing that could be directly applied to a successful romance. My parents are wonderful people, but their own marriage was a Fire Swamp that began with infatuation. Before they really knew each other, they'd already had a child, and their fiery union engulfed itself in conflict, leaving me without

a clear memory of them together and genuinely happy before they parted ways. I had no formative stories upon which
to visualize any future partnership. Many, if not most, of the
people I grew up with in New York City were also children
of divorce. Many of the children in the Buddhist community I grew up in also came from parents with difficult relationships. My parents' Buddhist teacher, who died the
same year *The Princess Bride* was released in theaters,
left behind a wife and family, but Chögyam Trungpa, as
brilliant as he was, was light-years from being a convention-
ally available husband or father. As a matter of fact, even the
historical Buddha himself, good old Siddhartha Gautama,
was a deadbeat dad. Perhaps that's blasphemous, but it's true.
He left his wife and infant son, seemingly without much
warning, and went off on his own. Like the rest of the spiritual world, the history of Buddhism, both ancient and
modern, is full of deeply wise people who suck at romantic
relationships. And that's okay.

I like to imagine that Siddhartha, responsible for a wife
and baby boy, had a panic attack and realized he no longer
wanted the life that had been created for him, or the life
he had co-created for himself. There is no historical basis
for believing he had acute anxiety. The story of Siddartha's
departure, even when he is appropriately humanized rather
than deified, is often told as a calm and collected decision
in response to his spiritual calling, a grounded choice to
pursue awakening in isolation from mainstream society.
Some accounts claim that his wife supported his choice
fully. Buddhist historians are quick to remind us that his
wife and son would later heartily forgive him for leaving,

and even become his disciples.[5] I prefer to think that Siddhartha simply freaked out at age twenty-nine (in possibly the most famous example of "Saturn Returns" in human astrological history) and fled his father's estate, at least in part because he couldn't handle his marriage or the pressure his dad placed upon him. Siddhartha's tale of awakening means more if he has real human obstacles through which to awaken. Personally, I prefer to share the stories of flawed but compassionate heroes. They're all I've ever known.

So, without any clear model, I was carrying around a hidden list of my ideal Buttercup's qualities. I took it with me to work, to parties and bars, on meditation retreats, to yoga classes, to volunteer events, to friends' art openings, to every café I entered. My eyes and heart darted and scoured, chasing connection and mirage alike. If in the period immediately before or after September 11 you happened to see a young guy recently out of college huddling in an urban café while carrying a book by Rilke atop a text on Mahamudra meditation, atop a book on post-structuralist theory, his eyes wandering beyond the page he was pretentiously pretending to read, trying to distract himself from his own pretending, thereby layering pretension atop pretense, combing the room for Buttercups . . . yeah, I was that dude.

My list of ideal qualities was an odd pastiche of references, a collage of images from *Harold and Maude*, Ngulchu Thogme's *The Thirty-Seven Practices of a Bodhisattva*, *Swingers* (sadly), Bob Dylan's "Visions of Johanna," LL Cool J's "Around the Way Girl," every high school and college crush I'd ever had, my mother (as both attraction and aversion), and of course Buttercup from *The Princess Bride*. Through my progressive education, and my mother's presence, I had been well schooled on the harm caused by objectifying women. But I had not learned how to stop longing for women as "other," genuine admiration toxically mixing with the need for possessive validation. Women were a missing piece, a completion, a companionship that seemed to offer both authentic connection and artificial status in a competitive world.

I could not bring myself to believe that "longing" for someone was at all, ever, in any way problematic. However, when I read some ancient Buddhist texts, they seemed to suggest (at least in the more questionable translations) that the desire I was repeatedly feeling was exactly that which needed to be extinguished. But I was, and am, a stubborn Buddhist romantic. For better or worse, I took my Buttercup list with me, in the back pocket of awareness, every single place I went.

Ethan's Buttercup List, circa September 11, 2001

- **BEAUTIFUL:** As sexy and "head-turning" as Robin Wright (or one of my other nostalgic crushes). The "beautiful" was for me; the "head-turning" was for my reputation.

- **EXACTLY SMART ENOUGH:** Not *Jeopardy* contestant smart, but able to banter and ambidextrously fence with every cultural reference I threw at her, but without being so smart that she'd make me feel stupid by throwing around lots of references I was clueless about.

- ❧ **CREATIVE:** She had to be.

- ❧ **SPIRITUAL:** Ready to join in long precoital conversations with deep "spiritual" gazes. And if she wanted to accompany me to a meditation retreat, bonus.

- ❧ **KIND:** Of course, of course, of course kindness mattered; kindness really *kind of* mattered to me when I was twenty-three.

At that period in my life, I had studied the ideas of nontheism and spiritual materialism. My intellect could repeat the idea that there was no savior from myself. I knew conceptually the problem with fixating on perfection. But anyone who has ever practiced mindfulness for two minutes can tell you that intellect and embodied experience are usually separate continents in the confused human experience.

I spent my first five to six postcollege years subtly comparing the women I met, dated, and failed to date, to the qualities in that list, oscillating between, on the one hand, deep loyalty to my ideals and, on the other, shame that I couldn't let my ideals go once and for all. It's amazing how fixated and aggressive a Buddhist can become when yelling at himself to *just let something go, damn it!* Just like aggressively shooing an uncomfortable thought in meditation, blindly hoping the thought will leave you alone for good only to watch it return, my own Buttercup fantasy kept coming back to me.

I wasn't so naïve as to expect to get everything. I knew that nobody gets their exact fantasy. Having it all, going big or going home, was an American myth, a Humperdinckian myth. Even before the experiment called America existed, getting everything you wanted was a Samsaric myth going back eons. It wasn't like *I* was Westley, the only man who possessed that Errol Flynn meets Ferris Bueller suaveness, funny and cunning enough to ride off on four horses with his perfect Buttercup and his perfectly eccentric friends.

Then, in 2006, seemingly out of nowhere, while recovering from a breakup, I met her: Buttercup of the East Village. She was a poet with a deep interest in art. She was smart and thoughtful. She cared about the world. We attended a MoveOn event together before we started dating, feeling good about contributing to communal activism and sanity during the "Dubya" era. She was even into yoga and Buddhism. And, by the way, not that it should matter—of course this shouldn't *ever* matter—Buttercup of the East Village was a former model who still did print work when she needed extra money.

In my personal experience, women don't usually make strong eye contact, at least not to express interest in a Manhattan Farmboy like me. I think it's due to the harsh objectification prevalent in our society, the ways that men who never learned better can make women feel uncomfortable with unwanted attention, with aggression that can make social spaces difficult and often dangerous for women to navigate with hearts open and gazes up. I often wonder what it would be like to be a woman, to enter each social space without being able simply to trust the genuine intentions of everyone I met. On all sides, our culture has made the work of letting us be genuine much harder than it needs to be.

In my teens and twenties, my mindfulness practice had a surprising side effect: it taught me how to be visually perceptive in a world of evasive intimacies and lightning-quick social cues. If I was in a social setting and wanted to know if a woman was sending me signals, I had to catch her in a split-second act. Not the act of looking at me, because eye contact was dangerous for her, but in the act of quickly looking away from me when I tried to make eye contact. If I caught a girl's eyes darting away, it meant that she may have—maybe, possibly, perchance—been checking this Farmboy out. I remember the moment I went to hear Buttercup of the East Village read her work at the Bowery Poetry Club. After she descended from the stage, I caught her eyes darting away from me, and it was on.

Buttercup and Westley fall (back) in love with each other when they tumble down a very steep hill together, a hill that Buttercup has just angrily pushed him down. There has rarely been a cinematic metaphor as direct as this one. Falling in love is a tumble both blissful and excruciating. As you tumble, your mind is focused only on the bliss; and after it's done, on the pain of the fall. In the case of Buttercup of the East Village, I'm not sure who gave the push, but I do remember that it was just that steep a plunge. Within one week of dating, we were spending six nights a week together. I would run out in the morning to get us each a coffee before my meditation practice, and would carry them back to her studio apartment near Tompkins Square victoriously, my grin wider than the diameter of my face. I would hum the tune of the Magnetic Fields song "The Luckiest Guy on the Lower East Side," feeling exceptionally literal about the lyrics. As I brought caffeine back to Buttercup of the East Village, I was finally, at long last, headed home—at least, that's how it seemed.

Within nine months she had moved in with me in Brooklyn. We had begun theoretical discussions of "ma-widge," but soon after moving in, she began having panic attacks with alarming frequency—soon, more or less every night. On top of the sleep deprivation we both developed, major cracks started to appear in our ability to communicate with each other clearly. Those cracks became fault lines, and the fault lines became earthquakes that shook me at a subterranean level, damaging my idea of partnership as salvation. This was an ideal that, yes, I could dismiss intellectually like any Buddhist Sherlock, but upon which my body and heart were still clearly fixated.

In the early days of our relationship, our miscommunications were invisible: we shared so much in a spiritual silence, so much that didn't even need to be stated, as we lay together *assuming* we understood each other perfectly. Why go hunting for all the ways in which our subjectivities might be at war with each other? But as time progressed, as the misunderstandings mounted, I felt increasingly irrelevant in the relationship. She began to panic, grasp onto, and then lash out at me more and more aggressively. In response, I found strategies to go numb, or to dive into my work, or else isolate myself in our small apartment next to the Williamsburg Bridge, which further triggered her own feelings of invisibility. This game of emotional dodgeball was no small feat for an urban couple. (Sometimes I practice compassion meditation for every unhappy couple who must engage in evasive maneuvers while living together in a seven-hundred-square-foot apartment.) Things went from bad to worse. And then things fell apart, which is what things do.

Now, there we were, two years later in the spring of 2008, in Tompkins Square Park, and I had chosen to say goodbye to Buttercup of the East Village, goodbye to that concept called "us." My meditation practice gave me a sense of clarity that, at the very least, helped me with not second-guessing a decision, even a painful decision, once it had been made.

Obviously, when a relationship ends, the person who breaks up is the privileged one, because they know what is coming. I have been on both sides, but in this case I took little solace in knowing I was the one who made the call. It was the most heartbreaking thing that had ever happened to me in the arena of romance, more heartbreaking than all the times I'd been dumped. The lessons I learned from Buttercup of the East Village, and the lessons I learned from the next five years of training on the high seas of dating, years that eventually led to my wife, could not have been more valuable to my spiritual path.

The Dance of Desire

OVER THE PAST SEVERAL THOUSAND years, many masters of the mind and heart have taken on the crucial, tricky subject of desire: how desire can lead to fixation, addiction, and self-destruction; how desire can be repressed; how desire can be sublimated into more socially acceptable or spiritually exalted forms. In the Tantric Buddhist tradition I inherit, many ceremonial practices are given over to the exploration of the relationship among passion, love, and awakening. We explore how the love between student and teacher can ignite a greater love for humanity and sentient beings, and also how the romantic desire of Eros can be alchemized into Agape, a 360-degree love, a form of compassion that explodes like a star, illuminating one's deepest connection with all sentient beings. According to Tibetan Buddhism, a human being feels a wide array of emotions, yet the one that most fully defines the human realm of experience is desire.

Unfortunately, across the millennia, desire has too often been viewed as a problem, rendered sinful, presented as nothing but a destructive emotion. Sadly, this denigration of desire has happened at the hands of both spiritual and psychological thinkers. Some very poor interpretations of Buddhist thought make the mistake of claiming that Buddhism believes desire to be the cause of suffering, the second noble truth. If this were true, then the elimination of both romance and chocolate chip cookies would be a good idea for your path of awakening. Once you got rid of all those things that might be a sensual trigger of desire, discarding all objects that might provoke uneasy feelings in your lower chakras and cause the brain to release dopamine or serotonin, you'd be all set. Unfortunately, the Buddha himself, during a period of misguided self-torture, discovered that this form of aggression toward a core human emotion simply does not work—ever. There are many things I don't know, but I do know this: the path of awakening is about the illumination of desire, not its exclusion.

It is true that in the first teaching the Buddha gave, he proclaimed the cause of suffering to be *tanha*, a word most literally translated as "thirst." It may seem that desire or attachment are suitable synonyms for this word, but *tanha* needs to be carefully contextualized in the body of teachings from which it originates, as well as lived within your own experience, for its meaning to be revealed. *Tanha*, as the Buddha described it, is not just a longing for a cookie or a person. Instead, it refers to the fixated need for the present moment to change into something other than what it is. *Tanha* means that *whatever* is happening in this moment, whatever the arising sensation, we either thirst for the experience to become permanent and stable, or else we thirst for the moment to cease to exist.

Tanha, therefore, describes a misguided fixation on the impossible. As Sakyong Mipham Rinpoche puts it, *tanha* can be described as "always wanting there to be another now." Obviously, because this wish is functionally impossible, our deeply engrained habit of trying to change what is already happening will cause suffering, creating recurrent friction between perception and reality. Suffering, *duhkha*, is not the nature of life, but a deeply engrained maladaptation to human experience. *Duhkha* describes the harmful friction between the actual moment and the fantasized moment. *Duhkha* is like the mind giving itself a rug burn, over and over again. Awakening is what happens when perception and reality become fully harmonized, when the tension between oneself and the present moment ceases.

So, what if desire is what is happening to you in the present moment? What if desire *is* your *now*? What if longing for another person, even intense and fiery longing, is simply the moment you inhabit? Is desire still suffering, then? No, not necessarily. Like any other emotion, desire is not inherently a problem, because desire occurs in the present moment, and the present moment is never inherently a problem. Needing there to be a different present moment is when we go astray. If you are naturally experiencing desire, then thirsting for desire to cease is just another form of suffering.

Of all possible emotions, desire is perhaps the most optimistic one. In its purest, energetic form, desire is a longing for connection. Something called "me" wants to join together (if only temporarily) with someone who is "other," or some object that is "not me." The beauty of this longing is that it naturally expands your private universe. In wanting connection, you begin to feel beyond yourself, yearning toward something vaster, more inclusive and interdependent. Within longing lives the seed of wisdom, a wisdom that wants to expand the range of lived experience beyond that which has already been experienced. That is why you long for that which is "other," because your inherent wisdom, your basic goodness, sees that there exists a much larger universe than the one you have already witnessed from your small vantage point. Inherently, there is neither sin nor confusion in this longing. Desire is the best thing that could ever happen to any of us. Desire is what fuels our ability to empathize. Without passion, there would be no compassion. Without desire, you have no chance at true love, and no hope of awakening.

Tantric Buddhist practices focus heavily on the transformation of desire. These tools examine how desire, in its confused state of grasping and fixation, can be transmuted into a more robust experience of love. In Tantra, this exploration includes both the sexual desire for another human and the more exalted forms of admiration we might feel toward a teacher or a guru. Western theorists, such as Heinz Kohut, have similarly focused on potentially positive aspects hidden in idealization: how admiring the positive qualities in an "other" can lead to integrating those positive qualities into yourself. Tantric Buddhism developed visualization techniques for imagining the support of spiritual heroes that could lead to feeling a full union with their heroic qualities. We use these techniques in order to realize that those same positive qualities, such as confidence and compassion, already lay dormant in our own minds. In order to awaken your love and confidence, you first visualize those qualities existing in another being (often a visualized teacher or enlightened archetype), and then slowly practice uniting your awareness with theirs.

In this way, desire, supported by mindfulness, will lead to positive growth. Longing is a solution to isolation and narcissism, a dissolving of a box-size universe in which there lives only an inadequate and insecure "me." A heart that is capable of admiring the qualities of another being is a heart that yearns to accommodate more, one that is ready to be touched by a larger world. Desire, if it manifests as connection, makes your universe bigger. But if desire leads to grasping and obsession, it can make your world very small indeed.

I always cringe when I read philosophers dissing desire or sexuality, because it always seems like they are disrespecting humanity itself. Desire is humanity's best friend. But it's a tricky friend, a friend you don't want to misunderstand. Desire is a little . . . well, high maintenance, to say the least. We work with desire by getting to know it, slowly and carefully. It behooves each of us to contemplate, with a touch of humor, the confusion we have already caused ourselves and others by not fully understanding the power of desire. It's a potential Fire Swamp of disappointment and addictive behaviors, and we need to know how to navigate its dangers. Desire is not a static thing. It's an ongoing movement between longing and discovery, separation and union, rejection and acceptance, regret and gratitude. If you bring mindfulness to the arenas of dating, romance, and partnership, you are implicitly declaring a willingness to dance with desire. If you don't understand the changing nature of this dance, you will repeatedly get burned.

Desire is a dance because desire is based upon, and always first experienced as, a state of separation. Much of the time, desire ends with outright rejection. Often, you aren't able to join with the object you seek. Someone already ate that last cookie, or someone hands you a cookie right after you've started your gluten-free, sugar-free (but never desire-free) cleanse. Or you work up the courage to press *send* on an awkward text message asking someone out for coffee, and they never bother to text you back. Most of the time, ladies and gentlemen, as I scoured the social arenas of the early twenty-first century, I did not catch *anyone's* eyes darting nervously away from me! When it comes to many desires, the universe simply responds to your earnest request with a cold "No. Sorry. Not *you*."

Desire offers no guarantee that the object of our desire will be available to us in return. Making friends with re-jection involves the realization that the world of objects and sentient beings cannot be controlled. Accepting rejec-tion becomes a crucial part of the dance of desire. If you don't accept that you can't control the wants of another person, or even control most of the inanimate objects you encounter, desire is only going to hurt. I am not a relation-ship expert, but I do know this: any attempt to manipulate another person into desiring you back, any "Game" you at-tempt to play to control someone's mind, is a karmic step in the wrong direction. When desire leads to an act of ma-nipulation, it is no longer wisdom but aggression. Aggres-sion might carry the illusion of control, but that appearance will be short-lived, and is bound to create more suffering.

Sometimes, beyond anyone's control, the stars do end up aligning for you. Buttercups and Studmuffins may ap-pear. This is when desire is experienced as a moment of union rather than separation. Union, or desire's acceptance, is where the dance of desire gets tricky. In your initial state of separation—when the "cookie" was just an idea outside yourself—you were hungry and unfulfilled. You expected the anticipated union to be the resolution of the longing, the end of the path. You thought that union with the object of desire would bring *satisfaction*. Instead, getting what you wanted now leads you into a new phase of feeling. Union doesn't resolve the previous moment of separation; it just creates a *new* moment. The way we view any object of desire from the perspective of separation is very different from how we feel after joining with it. The first time Buttercup glances at you across the room feels quite different from the moment you realize you feel claustrophobic around them.

Here's the tricky part about separation and union: you never actually get what you *wanted*. Instead, you *got* what you now *have*, which is a whole new experience indeed. Joining with the object of your desire does not satisfy the experience of desire. It only creates a new experience, as your perspective of the "other" shifts. Furthermore, what you now have inevitably changes, moving desire's dance forward into the next disorienting moment. Try this: slowly eat a cookie or other treat, and pay close attention, before, during, and after each bite, to how quickly your experience of pleasure and discomfort, union and separation, oscillates as the cookie disappears.

The confused mind, stumbling into the dance of desire blindly, often chases the "other" to alleviate the intensity of the physical feeling of desire, trying to make that overwhelming sensation cease, at least temporarily. If you've struggled to possess the "other," if you've searched a long time, or demonstrated courage to get to your "Buttercup," then the fact that you are now experiencing a new feeling, rather than the satisfaction of the initial desire, can be quite a disappointment, to say the least. We hope that getting what we want will be the story's end, which is where most rom-coms leave off. Instead, every union is just a new beginning, a next step in the ongoing dance between self and other, subject and object, separation and union, rejection and acceptance. And that's the biggest problem with rom-coms: they almost always end when the dance is just getting started.

At the point of union, you have two choices: you have to be willing either to dance with this new feeling of togetherness (a moment of "we" that comes with a slew of awkward and previously unnavigated intimacies) or to chase a new object of desire. If you are habitually caught up, tangled in cycles of *tanha*, always wanting there to be another now, then get used to disappointment every single time you reenter the chase. Samsara, the cycle of confusion, is based on perpetually finding another "now" to chase, and never understanding that the chase, as such, will never be complete.[6]

It all sounds so heavy. If we want to work with sexual and romantic desire, we need a bit of lightheartedness about the whole dance. We need language that makes the dance a little more playful. I would never have survived studying Buddhism without developing a sense of humor. Hence, Buttercup. The Buttercup myth perfectly caricatures the confusion of the romantic chase, and the disappointment that accompanies either the rejection or the fulfillment of our longings. Anyone who has ever gotten their Buttercup (or their chocolate cookie, for that matter) knows that the Buttercup you pursue is never the Buttercup you end up with, because your point of reference continually shifts as you dance with desire.

When you never learn your lesson, you enter a cycle of confusion, a samsaric state. In physics, cyclical motion happens because intentions and actions, force and velocity, are pointed in different directions from each other, and this discrepancy causes an object to spin around and around. Awakening from this cycle is not about suppressing desire, but rather about understanding that desire is a feeling that cannot, by definition, be satisfied by any chase. Mindfulness teaches us that feelings don't exist to be satisfied; they exist to be *felt*. Desire can neither be destroyed nor resolved. If you are going to be a romantic, you need to stay awake to desire's playful trickery.

When I joined with Buttercup of the East Village, I started to feel more and more misunderstood, because the stresses of intimacy changed my ability to idealize her, to fantasize about what her entry into my life represented. I'd left communication and friendship off my earlier Buttercup checklist, and now I was realizing that this absence was, simply put, not okay. Luckily for me, after parting ways with Buttercup of the East Village, over the next five years on the high seas, studying under a brutal guru called "modern dating," I experienced tons of chances to practice befriending desire.

Lost on the High Seas

Emptiness and Dating

> Only to the extent that we expose ourselves
> over and over to annihilation can that which is
> indestructible in us be found.
>
> —PEMA CHÖDRÖN

"I AM *NOT* THE FARMBOY! I AM THE DREAD PIRATE
Roberts!"

Forgive me. I think I yelled that out loud, and for the
second time, late one Saturday night. The first time, I was
addressing my friends, but the second, I was addressing
nothing but cracks in the sidewalk, tossed around by jet lag

and heartbreak. It was now three years later, the summer of 2011. I was standing outside a wine bar.

Have you ever looked back and wished everything had been simpler for you? The nostalgic quest for simplicity is a common feature of the best escapist fantasies. Everything would be simpler if the Farmboy could just be the Farmboy forever, remaining in a state of naïveté about his true love. If only the Farmboy had a trust fund, he wouldn't ever have to leave Florin. Everything would have been simpler if the Buddha—who *did* have a trust fund, so to speak— had never left his father's estate, if he had only been happy and awake right where he was. But the Buddha had a lot to learn about the mind and heart, and the Farmboy has a lot to learn about true love. Westley leaves home believing he has already found his true love, that their relationship will be safe until his return. He thinks he must leave to find his fortune in order to marry. In reality, he leaves home to have his ideals of romantic salvation compassionately destroyed somewhere out there on the high seas.

Westley's ship is captured by the previous Dread Pirate Roberts, and his warrior skills must be honed, sharpened by his fear of death and the abysmal probability of never seeing Buttercup again. He trains under the guidance of what can only be called, in Buddhist terms, a pirate guru. This brutal teacher tells him every night for a year, "Good night, Westley, good work. Sleep well. I'll most likely kill you in the morning."

After parting ways with Buttercup of the East Village, I was set loose for five years, about the same amount of time

Westley was at sea.[1] A lot happened during those five years. I watched *The Princess Bride* more voraciously than ever before, and even read the book twice. One minor event that complicated my dating life ever so slightly was being named a senior teacher in a Buddhist lineage at age thirty-two, in 2010. This appointment didn't affect my ability to date: my tradition has no celibacy requirements. In fact, the Shambhala teachings emphasize our need to be fully engaged in the society we live in.

Perhaps a small handful of contemporary practitioners will choose a celibate path. The most famous teacher in our modern lineage, Pema Chödrön, is a nun. Personally, I take to heart as much as I can the credo of my lineage: "Awake in the World." I measure the success of my practice by how well I am able to work with all the varied aspects of life in society. I have always believed that the fullest expression of a spiritual path involves a balanced engagement with the world. Career, art, culture, politics, friendship, sexual relationships, partnership, and family—all must become part of the journey. A classic Tibetan slogan says simply, "Train without bias in all areas." This meant, Sanskrit title or not, that I had to be as brave as any other Farmkid while sailing my little rickety ship upon the pirate-infested seas of modern dating.

During the five years between 2008 and 2013, I spent a great deal of time traveling. I taught Buddhism in what a friend jokingly refers to as the "Kale Belt," the wellness-oriented cities where a good kale salad and meditation have both seen skyrocketing popularity in recent years. Annually visiting places like Seattle, Portland, Austin, San Francisco, and Los Angeles, I had the opportunity to talk to lots of folks, heart to heart, about their spiritual paths.

There are many different methods for teaching Buddhism in both group and private settings. At its core, teaching is always a dialogue. (The original teachings of the Buddha, called sutras, are spontaneous dialogues between curious students and an open-hearted teacher.) Therefore, when I'm not guiding a form of meditation practice, teaching mostly means listening, listening to a lot of people open their own hearts and minds about what it means for them to perceive, feel, and relate to others. During these years, I spoke with thousands of people about how to bring love and heartbreak to the spiritual path. Romantic love remains painfully mysterious to most, if not all of us. When I was home in New York during this time, I dated. I discovered one crucial fact from my own experience and from working with so many others around the country. Whatever the current state of our romantic lives, we are all heartbroken—and that's not a problem.

Chögyam Trungpa Rinpoche spoke frequently about the "genuine heart of sadness," an awakened tenderness with which we may have lost touch. In our society, sadness is often viewed as a deficiency, a malfunction of the heart valve, a leak in the plumbing of our tear ducts. We don't give ourselves permission to be soft. We are often taught that sadness is a rupture that needs to be either hidden or fixed. But in the Shambhala teachings, our ability to access this "heart of sadness" is seminal to awakening humanity from its mostly dead state. For the warrior of compassion, sadness is no problem at all, no affliction, no mark of depression.

Instead, it is equal parts vulnerability and strength, a woundedness that comes from allowing our experiences to touch us, and a strength that comes from embracing, rather than defending against, the very vulnerability that intimacy uncovers. Genuine sadness is the real power source of every human connection: It is sad to fall in love, it is sad to fall out of love, sad to gain people's attention and then to lose it again. It is always sad to lose friends, lovers, and family. It is sad to watch children grow. It is sad to mourn someone's passing. And it is sad—oddly, poignantly, intensely sad—to lose a lover, not to the grief of death, but to the irreconcilabilities of relationships. There is nothing quite like breaking up—the pain of losing someone who remains alive and healthy, existing in the same world as you do. All this sadness is knitted into the fabric of the human condition. When you accept that sadness is a part of any relationship, it can begin to soften and sharpen you simultaneously. Sadness is your greatest strength.

It turned out that all of us interested in mindfulness—in the Kale Belt and beyond—were somehow heartbroken, though each heartbreak was unique. The etchings of wounds and insights were seared upon individual hearts so distinctly. We all shared a longing for meaningful connection. For many of us, this meant pursuing romance and partnership, and grappling with the complexities of that tumultuous pursuit.

During these same years, I was asked to officiate a series of weddings for friends and students, guiding them through ceremonies we co-created, usually a contemporary Buddhist (or, more accurately, Buddh-ish) ceremony that was a spiritual mashup: an homage to the couple's wishes to support each other and their familial lineages without a traditional religious ritual. Each time I officiated, I felt partly to mostly fraudulent because I was supposedly guiding the couple into a practice of relationship that I hadn't yet successfully taken on for myself. I, unfortunately, was no impressive clergyman. Not even close.

During this time, I became increasingly confident that spiritual teachings that suppressed or otherwise bypassed the human experience of desire were useless, perhaps even harmful, for my own journey, and therefore meaningless to pass on to fellow travelers on the path. When I was home in New York, I loved to see my friends. Luckily, I had some great Fezziks and Inigos in my life, both male and female. Their trust, generosity, and inspiration kept me sane on the path of teaching. My closest friends were good at undercutting my attempts at profundity with playful jabs. They helped me take on the challenge before me: to guide others down a profound path while still taking a "no big deal" approach to life. This mixture of profundity and no-big-deal-ness is the whole point of Buddhism.

Mindfulness asks that we cherish our moment-by-moment experience, treating each Tuesday morning and Saturday night alike as *extra*-ordinary. The challenge of awakening in day-to-day life is to treat both the holy and the mundane aspects of life as equally sacred. For me, this extra-ordinariness was hard to find alongside the subtle, often invisible shift in perception of those around you that comes with having a fancy Sanskrit title attached to your name. My best friends were priceless at keeping me grounded.

One summer Saturday night in 2011, I had just arrived home from the West Coast when I met up with a few Fezziks. We drank wine. Two of us were licking romantic wounds, lamenting more ships lost upon the high seas of dating. For me, another Buttercup litmus test had recently failed, the closest I had come to finding her in the three years since Buttercup of the East Village and I parted ways. This time, I had failed someone else's Studmuffin exam. Or maybe it wasn't me; perhaps bad timing, that true breaker of hearts across the eons, had failed us both. Now my friends were there to support me. I treated them to a diatribe explaining why I was no longer naïve about relationships. "Seriously, you guys," I claimed, "I've finally gotten over my *story line*." My rant was grounded in all kinds of Buddhist rhetoric, and in a frustrated critique of traditional Buddhism's failure to offer specific tools for navigating modern romantic relationships. "That's exactly what you should be writing about!" my friend said. She commented on how many classic Buddhist teachings focused on compassion in ways that were psychologically transformative, but how few classic teachings focused on applying compassion to, you know, specific relationships.

Classical Buddhism's universal approach is, we decided, its greatest strength as well as its greatest weakness. The more general a teaching becomes, the more universal its reach, yet the harder it becomes to discern the application of that teaching to a specific life experience. Compassion for all beings, check. Compassion for *this* being sitting across the table from you when you realize this second date isn't going well? Where is the ancient text that describes how to handle *that* situation? To ghost or not to ghost, that is the question.

We had to honor the teachings, but we agreed that we had to figure out this whole modern relationship thing by ourselves. Of course, a teacher or mentor or therapist might help, but they couldn't go on the date for us. Teachers couldn't fight duels of the heart for us. That evening, to keep my friends' attention, like the dork I am, I referenced *The Princess Bride*. I compared today's return to Brooklyn from the western Kale Belt to the Farmboy Westley's returning to his native country of Florin, not as a baby-faced serf, but as an accomplished pirate. Like a Buddhist master, the Man in Black was no longer fooled by appearances, no longer lured by shiny surfaces. He had found his edge, his precision. His mind was sharp, and please pardon my Sanskrit, but no one could fuck with the Man in Black—not Sicilians, not evil princes, and especially not manipulative sirens named Buttercup, temptresses whom the Man in Black had once mistaken for his true love. I was no longer naïve, either, I said. "I'm not the Farmboy anymore!" I exclaimed after a few glasses of wine, raising eyebrows and giggles at the table next to ours. "I am the Dread Pirate Roberts!" It was a night of lightheartedness, just what we all needed.

Eventually my friends left, but I wasn't quite ready to go home. I was jet-lagged, a state that made me simultaneously drunker and more awake than I intended to be at this hour.

I knew my parameters well, and I knew how to keep myself safe. But my heart wobbled out the door.

I walked out into an August night and felt the muggy air, content to be alone, wandering, observant. It was after midnight on a Saturday in Williamsburg, Brooklyn. Bars were crowded; people were drunk, sloppy, and loud, grasping after cigarettes and each other. Williamsburg had once again been transformed into the realm of hungry ghosts.

The Hungry Ghost Realm . . . of Dating

ANYONE WHO WANTS TO UNDERSTAND the desperation of modern romance should spend a post-midnight Saturday in a place like Williamsburg. Perhaps more than any other neighborhood in any other city, Williamsburg is the epicenter for the reemergence of the term *hipster* in the first decade of the twenty-first century, a sweeping identification that thrives on nondefinition. One thing is clear: the term is undoubtedly less visionary than its usage by the Beat generation and many others in the 1950s and '60s. For the vast majority of my twenties and thirties I have called this neighborhood my home base. Early on Saturday nights, it becomes an arena of hopeful desire, brimming with potential energy, the streets humming and thrashing with anticipation. It's as if thousands of desire batteries have all been charged to 100 percent and set loose upon one another. Early on a Saturday night, Williamsburg feels like a zone of heroic gods and goddesses. In order to experience its restaurants and bars, Farmkids wander from far-off kingdoms across the seas, places like France and Brazil. They even come from much more improbable kingdoms across *two* seas, such as . . . New Jersey. They come to locate their Buttercup or Studmuffin for the evening. Later, as the night wears on into intoxication and shipwrecked wishes, you can watch the streets descend into the realm of hungry ghosts.

"Hungry ghost" is a translation of an ancient Buddhist term, *preta*. It describes a psychological space where grasping has become an act of exponentially increasing desperation. This mental realm is composed of beings who have no relationship to their own confidence. They live in a *Mad Max* desert of their own making, chasing mirages, unable to satisfy or even feed themselves. The hungry ghost realm is considered a lower karmic realm. Karmic realms are not physical places per se, but rather collective states of mind. This means that the hungry ghost realm comes about due to a deeply obstructed sense of self. We become hungry ghosts when we lack self-confidence and run out of faith in our own resourcefulness. This leads to a cyclical grasping after the "other." As the desperation of this cycle increases, it creates exhaustion, a loss of trust in our resilience and ability to encounter what we need. As your reality becomes increasingly unsustainable, you chase hallucinations in a stripped-down desert. The hope of finding anything that qualifies as a long-term solution to dissatisfaction becomes increasingly frustrated, hollow, and illusory. But, out of habit, the chase continues, because chasing is all the hungry ghost knows how to do.

At last, in the particular hungry ghost realm of a late Saturday night out, there is no one left to call, no bar you haven't been to, no app whose membership you haven't swiped your way through multiple times. A moment like this, when hope is exhausted, would be a great time to practice loving-kindness meditation, if only you could remember to aim yourself toward caring thoughts. But the hungry ghost has not learned any of the contemplative techniques related to befriending oneself in solitude. Instead, you chase nostalgia—objects, people, or places that remind you of something that once upon a time gave you a fleeting feeling of satisfaction. And while chasing ghosts, you become one yourself—emaciated, depraved, and cynical about the possibility of true love.[2] To paraphrase Chögyam Trungpa Rinpoche, it is a fool who believes that he can possess his own projections, and the hungry ghost is the most destitute of all fools.

Without trust in basic goodness, we hope for either a temporary savior (to take the edge off our resistance to ourselves for a moment) or a permanent one (to save us from dealing with the mind in general). We grow increasingly susceptible to myths and holograms, the Buttercups draping themselves in red flags. This kind of hope, insofar as it makes us believe that any permanent saviors exist, is always illusory.

Going Beyond Hope:
The True Meaning of Emptiness

THE WORD *EMPTINESS* DESCRIBES A highly misunderstood body of Buddhist teachings. There are many ways to describe emptiness in philosophical terms, and none of them has to do with emotional black holes or the destruction of your sense of purpose. More than a metaphysical term, *emptiness* is best seen as an embodied experience, a glimpse of spaciousness in the midst of activity, an availability to the moment that comes about from the release of a rigid story line.

Now, a story line is something distinct from a story. Stories have a certain truth, although the perspective from which they are told alters their meaning. Each life has a story, and parts of my story are being relayed here. Your life has a story. It's not indulgent to tell your story; it is one of the main ways we pass along to one another the insights of human culture. We each experience a series of perceptions, thoughts, and feelings, events and relationships, and we share those, trying to connect and offer an insight or two.

A story line, however, is something very different. A story line is a recurrent thought that only exists in your mind, waiting to be uncovered and confronted in meditation. It's a cyclical narrative, a groove of thought stuck on a synaptic loop. Story lines create confining structures for how we think, act, and make choices. These loops tightly filter what we perceive, and also how we allow ourselves to experience other people's stories.

Examined and categorized by ancient philosophers from the Middle Way school, story lines usually have one of two basic structures, either of salvation (hope) or nihilism (fear). Often, a story line contains a bit of both. It's almost as if story lines are made of mental Velcro, of a stickiness that confines the flow of thoughts to a familiar direction. Looking for a solid point of reference, our story lines miss the fluidity of reality by latching on to one of these two extremes. Each story line overly invests in either hope or fear, reaching for some certainty to cling to, whether that certainty seems positive or negative, blissful or torturous. "If I get this job, I can afford a new apartment, and then I'll be all set" is an example of wishful thinking. Any story line of salvation ties permanent happiness to impermanent (and uncertain) causes and conditions. Anytime our worthiness as a human being has a big "if" attached to it, we are caught up in a story line of hope, an expectation that only disempowers us.

On the other hand, there are our fearful story lines, based on cynicism. Cynicism makes us fall into the trap of overgeneralizing painful and disappointing experiences from the past. "All politicians are corrupt" or "Nobody is ever going to look upon me the way Buttercup of the East Village once did" are examples of story lines based on fear, both of which have been synaptic loops caught within the mind of yours truly.

When pop culture leads us astray, its narratives cause whole groups, even whole generations, to invest in fixated story lines of hope or fear. Our rom-com culture gives us one huge aspirational story line, an undercurrent regarding what we idealize in romantic relationships. The rom-com story line usually involves the combination of hope for soul mate salvation and reaching for a higher social status in a competitive and unsafe world.

At the other extreme, our culture has many cynical story lines. We all know the cynic. The cynics arrive with their middle fingers blazing at all the naïve romantics out there. The cynic would rather vomit than hear someone regurgitate another soul mate fantasy. The cynic doesn't believe happiness is achievable, and says things like "Love is a fabrication of capitalism," while hosting anti-Cupid poetry readings in a basement on February 14. Cynicism often feels like a smarter bet than naïveté, because at least the cynic has started peeling away the falsehoods of wishful thinking.

For that hopeful Farmkid in all of us, the story line always involves an idealization of safety. Salvation story lines include one awakened feature: admiration. Admiration is the most crucial aspect of desire for another person because it brings you closer to basic goodness. In admiration, you see the good in another person and long to incorporate their qualities and presence into your own world. If you take that admiration too far, you end up mistakenly believing that your own worth relies on claiming ownership of that other person's goodness, their power. "If I just *got* this good situation" becomes "If I just *got* this good person," and you forget the essential fact that you can't take possession of another person's goodness. This is why you were attracted to that person in the first place, not to possess them, but to connect with another being who has a different perspective on the world. If you are going to avoid the hungry ghost realm in dating and partnership, your story line of salvation must be offered up for annihilation. My own dating life was a beautiful, uncomfortable practice of repeatedly watching my hopeful story lines perish.

I'll Most Likely Kill You in the Morning

"GOOD NIGHT, WESTLEY. GOOD WORK. Sleep well. I'll most likely kill you in the morning."

The Farmboy encounters a truly brutal guru, the previous Dread Pirate Roberts, who isn't the original Dread Pirate Roberts, just as there is no original warrior of compassion. The narrative of a brutal teacher is a classic one, woven throughout both Eastern and Western tales.[3] Despite his tough-love approach, it's pretty clear that Westley's guru cared for him deeply, because he surrendered his title and ship to Westley once the Farmboy's training was complete. With a good teacher, a lifelong practice of meditation can feel similar. If you meditate enough, if you drop your various story lines (both large and small) enough times, you begin to see impermanence more clearly. Impermanence is never a particularly comfortable truth to observe, at least not at first glance. Dropping even a small story line always feels a bit brutal, often like death itself. This is why meditation is never quite as pleasant as we "hoped" it would be. First you see the impermanence of perceptions and sensations, then you see the impermanence of the body, then the impermanence of thoughts and emotions, and eventually you begin to see the impermanence of your view of reality. The more you practice, the more it seems that there is this internal voice, full of humor and gentleness, saying, "Thank you for meditating. Good night now. Sleep well. I'll most likely kill your ideas about reality in the morning."

Luckily, my human teachers have always been exceptionally kind. I've never experienced even a moment of "brutal guru." They've never put me through any gauntlet where I feared my own death, although they do expect that I practice consistently, and that I keep showing up fully for the trainings to which I have committed myself. Without a doubt, my own master of brutality, the one who forced me to work with my fear of annihilation, was not a person but an activity. My own brutal guru was dating.

When you drop the story line of perceived hopes, you grow deft and skillful, because you begin to see the flexibility of any constructed ideology about who you think you need to be. Freed from the Velcro of the story line, you gain more room to maneuver. In the long run, this release will make you more flexible, more confident, and more capable of honest connection. Many of our perceived limitations are due, originally, to the constraint of a story line about reality. So when Westley reincarnates as the Man in Black, it's clear that his training with the previous Dread Pirate Roberts was incredibly useful. He is no longer the Farmboy. He is a warrior. And that warrior can do lots of things that seem inconceivable to the other characters, simply because he believes he can.

Of course, many profitable New Age spiritual messages make you believe that your story line is the *only* thing holding you back from success. These prophets of hope tell you that if you change your attitude or adopt a new mantra, everything you want will magically appear for you. We still have to deal with physical limitations as well as the limitations of others, and with the greater limitations of timing and coincidence. Believe me, it is more than just a story line that stops me from being able to dunk a basketball. Dropping the story line that I'm not good at basketball will not make me able to dunk, and anybody who tells you it will is selling something. Dropping my basketball story line just makes me able to show up on the court and see what happens. Given that romance is a game that no one really knows how to play, all you ever have to do is show up and see what happens. Nothing changes when you drop your romantic story line, except your willingness to be present. And if you are willing to be present, slowly but surely, things can start to shift.

When Pema Chödrön talks of annihilation, she is not talking about the annihilation of your body, or the annihilation of self-confidence, or the annihilation of belief in true love. She is talking about the process of a story line dissolving, a very limiting story line called "me." In meditation, as story lines dissolve with each breath, you begin to feel the indestructibility of the mind itself, the ability of your awareness to accommodate whatever might happen next.

Some mornings in my meditation, I notice some variation on the story line "Today is going to suck." In any meditation technique, you have the opportunity to submit your story line for a gentle annihilation, simply to let it be, and come back to the moment at hand, opening up to the direct perceptions of the moment embodied in a breath or a phrase of compassionate intention such as "May I be free from suffering." Story lines, when they become fixations, can turn into self-fulfilling prophesies.

Every time I sit down to meditate, I set an intention to drop at least one of my story lines. Some mornings, I feel clear and present; other days, my practice is plagued by nervous melodramas regarding unfinished projects, the e-mails yet to write, the parade of people I worry will be disappointed by my failures both imaginary and real. Sometimes my story lines include the fear of difficult conversations I need to have. Other times, they are full of regret for yesterday's missed opportunities or earlier life choices. "I wish I had become a painter instead" is one of my favorite loops of lament. I notice that thought, then drop the story line of escapist salvation and return to the breath, or else come back wholeheartedly to the phrase of compassion I am attempting to generate.

Dropping a story line is almost always uncomfortable. It represents something counterhabitual, a momentary cessation of the mind's engrained momentum. On a subtle level, story lines offer comfort similar to that provided by harmful physical substances. Learning how to drop a story line is one of the true redemptions embedded in mindfulness practice. When you drop your story line and come back to your senses, an amazing thing happens. *You survive.* For just a moment, you realize you don't need the narrative at all. All biological and mental systems work just fine without it. You can survive, perhaps even thrive, without provoking the claustrophobic loop of that thought pattern again and again. In surviving the annihilation of a story line, you gain a few extra drops of confidence regarding your mind's ability to deal with, and gain useful insight from whatever thoughts or emotions might come visit you next. This ability to survive the death of a story line is your real indestructibility, your awakened mind. Perhaps the best place I have ever found to practice dropping the story line, other than my meditation cushion, is while dating.

Dating Kills the Story Line

DATING IS A LOT LIKE a shared meditation. By showing up to the ceremony of a date with another person and treating it as a practice, you repeatedly let go of thought patterns stuck in a loop. With each new interaction, you get to watch beliefs about self and other rise and fall, rise and fall, and then wither away. If you drop your expectations, dating can be the best arena for witnessing story lines about what you are worth and what you need from another person. Only within their circular context can these beliefs convince you they are so necessary for your survival. When you drop the story line of salvation, you discover the indestructibility of your heart and mind. We call this discovery Buddha Nature. Anyone who goes out on a date would do well to remember the Buddha Nature of both participants.

Here's how I survived my time dating: I finally came to view dating as a practice, and not just any practice, but the ultimate practice of dropping the romantic story line, my Buttercup myth. Just like in meditation practice, I had to drop my story line on dates and in relationships, again and again and again. Repeatedly dropping the Buttercup story line over time allowed me to show up a little more open-heartedly, chancing the possibility of a new connection.

Nothing, and I mean *nothing*, that happens in the

process of dating has much to do with whatever any of us expected to happen. Let's be honest, from the standpoint of our hungry ghost tendencies, dating is a nightmare. For the hungry ghost, a date is the meeting of two zombies, each attempting to cannibalize the other's basic goodness, each craving deliverance from the recurrent feelings of rejection and conditional happiness that never seem to land anyone exactly where they hoped. If you are caught up in a story line, then dating is a festival of painful projections.

Each new interaction brings your story line about your own desirability and worthiness right up to the surface. If you treat every rejection and miscommunication as yet another wave crashing against your confidence, you will be swept overboard quickly, drowning in resentment and sorrow. And if your story line includes the toxic and self-torturing belief that you should already be an expert, that you should know how to do this relationship thing by now, even though many of history's greatest spiritual masters were themselves rendered clueless by romance, then you are going to quickly become a cynic.

Perhaps, in an enlightened society, where human dignity is reaffirmed within more compassionate and caring social rituals, each date would start with a bow, a mutual acknowledgment of each other's basic goodness. The first thing you might say to each other is "So, this is really hard, right? Let's try to be decent humans to each other, okay? I promise that I will not hungry ghost on you. Please don't hungry ghost on me." Dropping your story line and showing up, opening yourself to the possibility of *either* connection or rejection, is about the most transformative thing a human being can do.

Return to the Human Realm

THE DESTRUCTIVE GRASPING OF THE hungry ghost realm doesn't only create metaphorical effects, but also conditions our cultural experience. One of the most powerful ways to understand interdependence is to see how the mind and the outer world slowly come to reflect each other. Human minds, and the shared culture that those many minds create together, are completely interdependent, which is why we never meditate alone. As I write this, stories of sexual assault against women mount, creating a shockingly pervasive "rape culture" that has unfortunately affected many of my own female friends. The hungry ghost culture has also affected many of my male friends in a variety of harmful ways, as we fall prey to the destructive myth that the way to get what you want is through physical or psychological aggression and gaslighting, either toward another person or toward your own being. And then there are all the various manipulations at work in the porn industry.

Even when no physical violence is present, the hungry ghost realm still pervades this world. Romance is widely viewed as a profit-maximizing commodity, something for which to design a new app. Weddings are not simply a ceremony of community, but an excuse for vendors to jack up their prices. At our worst, our entire world has become fooled by narratives of romantic and sexual salvation, crafting a culture that all too often values the myth of possession over the process of connection. Mindfulness is what allows us to bring romance and sexual desire back into the human realm.

I remember wandering the streets of Williamsburg into the wee hours that summer night in 2011, witnessing interactions rather than participating in them. My mind leaned back into a careful observation of a more privileged subsection of the human race, a group that included me. The streets were still vibrant with people, and their passion batteries still had just a little juice left, charges amplified by fermented substances, running on fumes of intoxication. These people were sacrificing tomorrow's equanimity for tonight's desperation. Thankfully, some people I witnessed seemed fully content, lucidly present and awake with friends or lovers. Others were still up in their god realms, flirting their faces off within bubbles of bliss, bubbles doomed to pop, because that's what bubbles do. Some people were in hell, arguing painfully with each other in public, even coming to drunken blows. Some hungry ghosts were salivating, chasing Buttercups, a fantasy that dissolved as last calls approached once again at bars. Maybe some people were chasing the much deeper myth we all chase, the fairy tale that it might be possible to avoid dying alone, stuck with our oldest frenemy, our own minds.

There's another, brighter side to this sad story, one that coexists with the tragedy of the hungry ghost realm: the *true* hopefulness of being a human, the possibility of seeing desire as an opportunity to awaken. Real hope lies not in salvation, but in connection. No matter how insecurely we chase ghosts, we are still human, and humans can always return to the present moment and connect with each other. I saw this side of our culture, too, as I wandered the late-night streets of my neighborhood. Many people were thriving in the human realm, celebrating their connections. For many, Saturday night was a way to let go of the fantasies of work and status and just show up, to celebrate with each other. There is no reason you can't be a warrior of compassion in the field of romance. There is no reason that even Brooklyn, that hipster kingdom, can't become an enlightened society, too.[4]

Eventually I arrived at home that night. I felt more clear than ever before that Buttercup had always been a dream. I spread out, by myself, in bed. I slept well, and in the morning I reincarnated, arriving once again into the day. Before I meditated, I opened my laptop and watched *The Princess Bride* for the nth time, content this Sunday to watch it all alone.

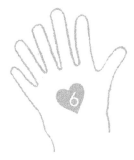

Basic Goodness

How the Farmboy Was Finally Reborn

> You be careful. People in masks cannot be
> trusted.
>
> —FEZZIK

IN ESSENCE, WESTLEY'S STORY IN *THE PRINCESS*
Bride is a reincarnation tale. You could say that Westley
reincarnates twice: once upon the high seas, under the direction of his pirate guru, to let go of the Farmboy's naïve
hope of salvation. The second time is far more literal, as he
returns from his mostly dead state with some help from

his friends, in order to let go of the Man in Black's obsession with the other kind of story line, the cynic's narrative.

Reincarnation is a hard concept to consider literally. When it came to such topics, ones that could not be verified by experience, Chögyam Trungpa used to say something that is, surprisingly, also a line in *The Princess Bride*: "Your guess is as good as mine."[1] People are often surprised, considering how scientifically grounded and psychologically relevant Buddhist thought appears to be, when someone starts talking about reincarnation as if it were fact. This topic seems to be a big departure from the more experiential "touch it, feel it, taste it" approach implied by a life of mindfulness. Many people have told me how much they admire Buddhism . . . except for reincarnation.

Certainly, one way of looking at reincarnation is mystical, religious, and distancing to our secular beliefs. It posits a relationship between the continuity of consciousness and observable physical matter that isn't scientifically provable. Reincarnation can lead to all kinds of story lines that need to be dropped about which sage, hero, or celebrity you might have been in a past life. At the same time, the theory that your consciousness simply ends when you die, the main premise of scientific materialism, is also not provable. I am agnostic when it comes to any literal interpretation of reincarnation. Anybody who presumes to know what happens after death without a method of testing their hypothesis is making an unscientific assumption, including materialists who claim that consciousness is completely reducible to the physical brain. Better, here and elsewhere, to hold the space of uncertainty.

There is another way to think about reincarnation, a way that avoids unverifiable claims in either direction, a way that is much more accessible to our lived experience and doesn't require mysticism to make itself practical. Consider reincarnation a Buddhist plot device, one we use to describe both the continuities and discontinuities of identity. Have you ever gone to bed stressed out and caught up in anxiety, and then gotten a good night's sleep, or just talked to somebody you trusted, or practiced a little bit, and woken up the next morning feeling refreshed and liberated, like you were still you, but that "you" was in a different situation, like something unnamable had lifted or shifted? Waking up in the morning is an act of reincarnating to your daily life. In a sense, every single present moment is an unheralded reincarnation, an interplay between continuity and discontinuity, chains of causality mingling with gaps of spontaneity.

When you pay attention, the relationship between the current now and past and future moments is quite tenuous. We know that the present moment exists in reference to the previous one, but the present is never actually defined by the past. There is always a gap, a break between the momentum of the past and the trajectory of the future. In that gap of nowness, the experience of yourself and your world is in a constant process of rebirth and possibility. This way of considering reincarnation isn't even metaphorical; within this one lifetime, reincarnation happens constantly. Our bodies are in a constant state of regeneration as cells replace themselves over and over, until we are literally composed of brand-new material. Our minds are visited by a recycling of views, preferences, and opinions. Yet there is some miraculous connection between the "me" that existed in 1987 and the me that exists in 2017. If you are paying attention, the present is always inhabited by a new "you."

Taken this way, reincarnation is never proposed as data-driven truth, but rather as a way to personally investigate the aspects of our human experience that are continuous and consistent, alongside those aspects that are spontaneously shifting, open to reinterpretation. In Westley's case, this reincarnation of identity happens twice. He first learns that he can't just be a naïve Farmboy, especially not when it comes to true love. To surrender hope of salvation, he has to confront impermanence directly. He has the former Dread Pirate Roberts to thank for this first rebirth as the Man in Black.

But he's not done. Westley's second reincarnation, his return from his "mostly dead" state, is what lets him experience true love. In order to fully connect with another person, we all need to overcome the ways our hearts have gone numb. Just as the rom-com gives us a story line of salvation, modern culture gives us a very cynical story line, and it is this acquired contempt for optimism that we must overcome.

The Final Reincarnation: Dropping the Cynic's Story Line

SOMETIMES IT SEEMS OUR WORLD has been surrendered to the cynics. In culture, news media, politics, art, storytelling, and romance alike, it often feels that optimism has become synonymous with fluff, cliché, and stupidity. Tell anyone to look on the bright side, and you will get many an eye-roll. Good news is rarely clickbait; the bad news and fearmongers catch more views. Obviously, there is good reason to err on the side of pessimism. The oceans are rising. Racism, violence, and inequality abound. Some politicians really *are* corrupt, and our leaders appear more like humorless versions of the bad guys from *The Princess Bride* every year. It also makes sense to be cynical about relationships. By any standard, most relationships simply *don't* work out. Much of what is presented spiritually is demonstrably bullshit, clichéd recipes for wisdom, when real wisdom can only be uncovered through direct experience. So, yes, our cynicism is understandable, but that doesn't mean it isn't an extreme belief.

When your trust is shipwrecked, the sense memory of the pain of betrayal makes you not want to fall into similar traps ever again. You become terrified of blind spots; you learn strategies to avoid anything that reminds you of old wounds. The heartbreak and grief of things not turning out the way you expected make you want to stay as far from optimism as you can. Out of this aversion, you begin to find strength in attacking optimism, defending yourself from pain by going on the offensive against all the inauthenticities of the world. The cynic discovers the sharpness and power found within a critique of *other* people's story lines. But this addiction to perpetual critique is just another way to avoid feeling, a way to cling to the certainty of numbness, and to avoid the vulnerability of living in an uncertain world.

Our culture often assigns the highest intellectual ranking to the critic, the person most capable of slicing through
the naïve story lines of others. If you can demonstrate someone else's hypocrisy, or tear someone's misperception down
to size, or troll someone's ego with the best of memes, then
you might claim the prize of smartest person in the (virtual) room. For the person who has lost hope in humanity,
this sharpness might be the best remaining chance for
happiness. Cynics can't be messed with, because they cut
the world before it can cut them (again), avoiding vulnerability by stabbing through the falsehoods of others.

Skepticism contains tremendous accuracy. After all, every
relationship is defined by the boundaries of death, either
the death of the body—the best-case scenario, according to
any model of romantic longevity, is that you make it all the
way "until death do you part"—or the death of an identity,
a particular incarnation of who you are and what you want.
(This sort of death is what often happens in a breakup.)
My history with romance, my family and lineage histories,
alongside my study of the teachings of impermanence—
all these gave me much to be skeptical about when it came
to creating a successful relationship.

The rom-com myth takes its toll on all of us. Disappointed
by false idols, the mind understandably careens toward the
other extreme, the cynic's apathy and nihilism. We become
edgy and doubtful about finding any joy, a place to be ourselves, cynical about the prospect of belonging to any workable relationship. Our thoughts take on a structure defined
by belief in negative permanence. *Things are bad right now,*

they're always going to be bad, and as far as I can remember,
they always were bad. In this realm, not only is Buttercup a
myth, but so is any sense of meaning. In this more depres-
sive extreme, we chase a different set of ghosts. We make
choices based on a kind of self-destructive irony.

If we can't have something ideal, we think, then at
least we can have something painful enough to qualify as
masochistic profundity, our own private dystopia. After all,
these days, who doesn't prefer dystopia to utopia, *Blade
Runner* to Walt Disney? "Look at all those pretty red flags,"
we say, not even sure if we're being sarcastic anymore, not
worried if our choices lead only to pain.[2] Yes, we let go of
our hope of a savior, but this tearing down of optimism is
no more truthful to our experience than the myth of saviors was. The cynic, the Man in Black, is just as extreme as
the Farmboy, even if the cynic resides in the culturally
cooler of the two extremes. Salvation and cynicism are both
just story lines. Both must be recognized, befriended, and
then released, again and again and again.

As I ventured further into dating, the volume rose on
the voice of my inner cynic. Each time there was a miscommunication, each time there was a rejection, each time I felt
either smothered or forgotten, each time I heard of a friend's
partnership collapsing into a messy rubble of resentment, I
could choose to tell myself that nothing was ever going to
work out in the end. Furthermore, I could even use the Buddhist teachings on impermanence and emptiness to bolster
my skepticism in a preemptive "Buddha told you so" kind
of way. I refer to this preemptive quasi-Buddhist cynicism

as "impermanence sabotage." I could always find, or construct, a spiritual quote to demonstrate that things not working out was simply the nature of samsara, the result of the cycle of confusion and projections that couldn't be satisfied. We could even use the inner cynic to become dismissive of self-care, sabotaging the wellness of mind and body under some false belief that health is impermanent, and that therefore taking care of ourselves is just too big a burden.

It is true: nothing is going to "work out." Or, rather, whatever does work out will eventually come unraveled. That's the fluidity of impermanence at work. All that is born will die. All that is solid melts into air, and all that is holy will be profaned, as Karl Marx famously wrote. There is literally nothing to hold on to. You win, impermanence. You will always win.

This is an important message, one that the former Dread Pirate Roberts teaches Westley very well. You're going to die. No savior, no fairy tale, and if I don't kill you tomorrow, something else will. All romance ends in death, all expectations will be frustrated, and all hungry ghosts will keep on chasing their projections until they exhaust themselves and finally get the message. If you are going to chase your hopes, to try to use a relationship to escape from yourself, then please, please, please, for the good of everyone, get used to disappointment.

Buddhism is a great tradition for religious skeptics who still yearn for an ethical and psychological framework to guide them. Perhaps this is why Buddhism continues to catch on in our increasingly agnostic and atheistic era. The dharma implores us to sharpen our swords and be honest about what helps and what harms, both ourselves and others. The teachings on ethics are meant to be pursued in a trial-and-error manner, and when you discover a view that doesn't work, you offer it up for its own dissolution. It was exactly this kind of take-no-prisoners approach to looking at one's own experience, this kind of invitation and even encouragement to skepticism, that attracted me to Bud-dhism as a teenager.

In my sophomore year of high school, still resentful about the collapse of my nuclear family, I read Chögyam Trungpa and Thich Nhat Hanh's interpretations of emptiness. Their writings were commanding, as if they had sharpened their own swords, and yet their words didn't seem dogmatic. They weren't telling me what to think. Instead, these teachers left tremendous space for the skepticism that I felt toward matriculating into a world of cultural constructs and rules, rules that often seemed random at best, yet were sometimes presented like absolute truths. Buddhist thought gave me a safe arena in which to fence with all my feelings of disenfranchisement. My favorite Buddhist text regarding dropping the story line was, and still is, a pithy, and quite famous, commentary called the Heart Sutra.

In this short dialogue, a sort of Cliffs Notes (or the "heart") of a much longer body of teachings, a conversation takes place between two of the historical Buddha's senior students. Meanwhile, the Buddha sits quietly and listens. One of his students completely deconstructs everything the Buddha has taught them so far, demonstrating that any spiritual teaching is simply a conceptual mapping, a signpost, a signifier of approximate meaning. No teaching is without context, and outside their appropriate context, the concepts found in any spiritual teachings will *always* forfeit their meaning. After this dialogue, in which Siddhartha's sacred words have been literally trashed while he sits quietly listening, trashed by his most cherished students no less, the Buddha applauds and validates his students' skepticism.

In other words, in this text, the founder of a spiritual tradition listens to his most senior student decimate everything he has taught so far, and then expresses deep gratitude to the student for doing so! For a leader to be able to do that takes an enormous depth of self-confidence, an ability to accommodate skepticism as a necessary tool of growth. My teenage thought at reading this text was simple: the Buddha was fearless. Or, in the vernacular of 1990s New York City: the Buddha was *dope*.

There is a subtle difference between being a skeptic and being a cynic, although they do share one crucial weapon: a bullshit detector. In classic Tibetan Buddhism, this BS detector is symbolized, surprisingly, by weaponry, usually swords, sometimes arrows or spears. Swords are everywhere in Himalayan Buddhist art, and they represent the skeptic's ability to slice through *his own* confused ideas about reality.

It is good to give your inner skeptic a voice, just enough to keep you honest, just enough to make you able to wield the sword of discernment. When the Man in Black emerges on the screen, it is clear he's learned cynicism's power to sharpen the mind. His dialogue is even greater than his fighting skills. But he's also a cynic, and his bitterness makes him unwilling to admit the real truth at hand: that he wears a mask to cover a broken heart.

If nothing can mess with you, it means nothing can touch you. If you wear a mask, you can always perform, but you can't connect. We set aside one night a year for this purpose. But outside costume parties, masks only serve as a defense mechanism. Skepticism, on the other hand, is an unmasked, naked inquisitiveness. Skepticism demonstrates true curiosity, a willingness to live without swallowing easy answers to life's tough questions. But cynicism is something else. As the great sage Fezzik notes, "People in masks cannot be trusted." For me, this is *the* most important line of the movie, one of the greatest spiritual lessons I have ever received.

The biggest problem with cynicism is that you still have to exist in the world. Despite possessing a seeming preference to remain forever sidelined, perpetually trolling the perceived shortcomings of others (a great strategy to avoid failing yourself), the cynic inevitably has to make choices. Our most cynical choices are based on a different kind of story line, a narrative that takes the form of the apathetic mantra "nothing really matters." This mantra usually manifests in acts of materialism. The materialist privileges disposable pleasure above the cultivation of qualitative shifts in habit, preferring instant gratification over long-term connection with self and others. The logic of materialism's story line is this: "If nothing really matters, I may as well just get prowess or pleasure. If I find the best way to feel good, or else the best way to self-destruct, the prettiest red flag to wrap myself up in, then I will forget my discomfort for one moment. I will learn to escape the sadness that my romantic worldview, my longing to connect with others, hasn't worked out the way I wanted." As William Goldman himself wrote, "Cynics are simply thwarted romantics."

When we meet the Man in Black, he is light-years from being naïve. As he summits the Cliffs of Insanity, he is brilliant, so cynical it's not funny. After all, he's pretty sure his love has sold out on him for both wealth and comfort. In this space, his wit and sword are both razor-sharp. "Get used to disappointment," his veritable battle cry before his first sword fight, could be the mantra offered at the start of any meditation retreat, at least if you think the practice might offer some kind of self-transcendence. No matter how much you meditate, you will still be you. If we think we're going to gain a new, better version of ourselves, how disappointing is the realization that there's no way to escape who you really are? No matter how much you try to escape your ordinariness, you will never get away from yourself, and as far as any spiritual narrative of blissful transcendence goes, that fact is the ultimate disappointment.

Westley has been hardened by the (perceived) abandonment of his true love, and trained by his Dread Pirate guru, yet his heart remains closed. He is so armored that he even turns sarcastic toward his love, snarkily claiming to have killed Westley himself—"Once word leaks out that a pirate has gone *soft* . . ."—and when she tells him to stop mocking her pain, he says the very famous words "Life is pain, Highness. Anyone who says differently is selling something."[3]

This line is almost the most Buddhist line of the whole film. *Almost.* But it is off by one word, and the absence of that word illuminates a very common misunderstanding of the Buddha's teaching on the truth of dissatisfaction, or *duhkha.* This misunderstanding creates a subtle deviation away from dharma and into nihilism. If Westley had said, "Life *includes* pain. Anyone who says differently is selling something," he would've been perfectly attuned to reality, grounded in a blend of honesty and compassion, free from the extremes of hope and fear. If, furthermore, he had said, "The attempt to *exclude and ignore the inevitability of pain is what causes us to suffer,* Highness," then he would've been practically giving a dharma talk.[4] But he's not ready for that. First, this Man in Black must unmask, which rekindles his longing. Then, to overcome the cultural negativity of the kingdom in which he lives, circumstances dictate that he must reincarnate one more time. Westley has to find a way to recover the Farmboy's belief in true love. And he can't do it alone.

It's not Westley's fault that he winds up in a mostly dead state, just as it's not our fault that the shattering of hope turns us into trolling cynics who doubt everyone's intentions and ridicule the goodness of this world. Sometimes the world we have inherited leads our experience into dark corners, from which it is scary to emerge. Just as Humperdinck and Rugen get in the way of true love's fulfillment, our culture gets in our way, and our path to openness is longer and more winding than we hoped.

Basic Goodness, Recaptured

IN THE SHAMBHALA TRADITION, THERE is one quintessential way to take off your mask, and it is something we do again and again throughout the path, using a variety of personal and interpersonal methods of inquiry. All these methods have one common feature: they each present a messy process of contemplating, questioning, wrestling with, feeling unworthy of, glimpsing, and slowly arriving at a greater trust in the truth of your basic goodness.

There are many ways that basic goodness can be investigated, many synonyms or experiences that can point you toward a meaning that can be only approximated by language. Two main contemplations of basic goodness have helped me reincarnate beyond hope and fear. The first has to do with overcoming the first story line, the need for salvation.

Sakyong Mipham Rinpoche describes basic goodness as the experience of *worthiness*. When you inhabit your basic goodness through practice, you feel suddenly confident, worthy of being alive, and willing to just be as you are. You can take up an appropriate amount of space on planet Earth, because you are one of its rightful inhabitants. Claiming your spot on Earth is called "taking your seat" and the meditation posture directly reflects confidence in your worthiness to take up space. Basic goodness is like a passport that verifies your citizenship in the human race.

Feeling unworthy and lacking confidence, not wanting to take up space, presents an unfortunate irony: the less worthy we feel, the more space we tend to take up, because we have to chase a whole bunch of "others" in order to feel like we belong. This is the tragic irony of self-obsession. Worthiness has nothing to do with arrogance or ego. It's not about misguided attempts to be the "best." Worthiness is how you overcome the salvation myth and stop being a hungry ghost—you realize that *you* yourself possess qualities of admiration. When admiration for others and the realization of your own admirable qualities become equal participants in your worldview, that's when you can really take your seat.

One of the universal characteristics of being an attractive person is appearing as if you don't *need* attention. In this world of hungry ghosts, the one who is not chasing any salvation becomes increasingly sought after, because the rest of us wonder what it is you've managed to figure out. Sometimes this confidence is misperceived, and you end up attracted to people who aren't really confident, just distant. One way to project false confidence is to space out completely. The pretense of apathy is a false worthiness, that "I don't even care so I might not get back to you for a month" state of mind. That's not confidence; that's avoidance. Real confidence is how we overcome our story lines of hope.

The other synonym for basic goodness I love to contemplate is this: *innocence.* What if humans, at our foundation, are innocent of any fundamental wrongdoing? Perhaps this view seems too optimistic. How could we explain Hitler, or police brutality, or, for that matter, a mean-spirited ex-lover, in terms of basic goodness? The Tibetan phrase for basic goodness could also be translated as "original purity."

No matter what mistakes you've made, no matter what confusion you have been caught up in, you can always return to your innocence and see things freshly, through the eyes of a child. You can always get back to the source of your humanity, a spring from which there is no fundamental corruption.

Innocence is not some naïveté that pretends there aren't problems or reasons to be skeptical. Basic goodness is often mistaken for "it's all good," some saccharine platitude. We can't be spoon-fed basic goodness without questioning it, informed as we are by years of remembered let-downs and confusion. And you should question it. Basic goodness is waiting for you to struggle with it, every day. But the voice you use to ask the skeptic's questions ought to sound like the voice of an intelligent child, not an Internet troll. Each time you meditate, you can take that fresh curiosity and apply it to those same old thought patterns you're so sick of. Similarly, each time you go to a movie, you need to remember what it felt like to go to a movie theater for the very first time. And each time you connect with a new romantic interest, you could remember what it felt like before you grew jaded by the process of innocently connecting with another human. Seeing every moment as fresh is the only way to conquer the cynic's fearful narrative.

Here is the riddle of enlightenment in relationships: How could a person move through the world with total savvy, complete confidence that she knows her own experience and won't be fooled by anyone's silly games, yet still be curious, perceiving openly with the eyes of a child? Can innocence also be cunning, and vice versa? Can you walk down each street in life knowing you've been down this block before, and still walk with a clean gaze and an open heart? You know you've seen it all, but you let every new experience be brand-new. This innocent savvy, this middle path between hope and fear, creates the ideal conditions for discovering a healthy relationship.

I believe that a master warrior lives within this riddle. The awakened romantic is never fooled by appearances, but they are curious about what a fresh connection might bring. The only way to move toward this balance is to carefully spot both story lines, the naïve and the cynical. Sometimes you'll need to unsheath your sword to cut through false saviors, yes, but you also need to move through the world unmasked, with innocence rediscovered.

Coming Back to Life

WHO HELPS WESTLEY WITH HIS final reincarnation? Appropriately, he is brought back to life by the movie's only example of a successful long-term romantic relationship: Miracle Max and Valerie. Just as every character in this work displays their eccentricities, Goldman's portrayal of a successful marriage deviates spectacularly from storybook norms. Yet this argumentative pair are the ones responsible for the Farmboy's miraculous rebirth. It's almost as if Max and Valerie are saying, "Is this what you want, kiddo? This what you are looking for? A real relationship? With your Buttercup? Do you want all the difficulties and tough times we've had, both together and alone? The times we can't stand each other? The times managing each other's depression? Do you want a relationship in the trenches? To watch what decades of gravity do to each other's bodies? You want the disappointments, the arguments, the hair-pulling confusion? Is this what you crisscrossed the seas to find? Here it is, Farmboy, come back and get it. All you have to do is stop being mostly dead. All you gotta do is wake up." And Westley does.

Is your own story of rebirth ever complete? Is completion even a possibility? Maybe. Or maybe the work will never be done, because the story lines of salvation and cynicism might maintain some hologram-like presence in your thoughts, depending on how your journey proceeds. To get caught up in a story line is as human as getting free of one. Perhaps awakening is not about hope and fear disappearing from the mind. Perhaps it is about those narratives becoming less and less sticky as we recognize them with increasing wisdom. As awareness becomes more prominent, we get caught less often, until our old story lines become friends and confidantes, minor characters and color commentators, rather than demons.

An awakened master uses hope and fear in a new way. A Buddha, I believe, has transformed hope into a kind of aspiration, an intention without expectation. A Buddha has transformed cynicism into a knowing skepticism, never accepting easy answers or prostrating before false idols. In some versions of the Buddha's life, his inner traps of hope and fear were embodied by the character of Mara, an enticing demon who kept trying to undermine Siddhartha's self-confidence and discipline. After his complete enlightenment, Mara didn't disappear from the Buddha's life. Mara kept on visiting the Buddha, just to say hi, just to have some tea together. I often like to think of my own inner voices of hope and fear as another duo from the 1980s, those good old Muppets in the balcony, Statler and Waldorf.

What does it mean to be brave when you approach relationships? It's interesting that we use the word *warrior* in the Shambhala tradition, since in Sanskrit, the word literally means "hero friend," and the Tibetan literally means "brave one."[5] The not-quite-literal translation "warrior" is an attempt to reclaim the meaning of bravery from those who incite violence, to proclaim the bravery that it takes to overcome confusion. Ideally, being a warrior involves no violence. When, at the film's conclusion, Westley implicitly tells Inigo that he could become the next Dread Pirate Roberts in his own wacky way, he is describing the pirate not as a person, but as a lineage, as a placeholder identity passed from one warrior to the next. The Dread Pirate is now clearly a tradition of those who share their training through hope, fear, and comedy.

When you open beyond hope and fear, that's when the warrior is most ready to connect with another person. I have no idea who you will meet when you hold this balance, or if you are even interested in that sort of relationship. I know a lot of people who feel ready to meet someone and still feel somehow marooned in the cosmos. "I'm working so *hard* to be present and open, but nothing's working." I know exactly how that feels. A good relationship comes from more than just your readiness. It's about timing and connection. There's not that much you can control, but I do know that if you drop the rom-com story line and unmask your inner cynic, if you contemplate both your worthiness and your innocence, it won't really matter who you meet. You will be on the way to a more awakened relationship with your own mind, and that's what matters in the end.

From the first moment you investigate the possibility of a connection with a new person; to the sad rejection of not getting your text returned;[6] to the nerve-racking excitement of going on a date, trying to present yourself as a respectable, perhaps even noteworthy, human being; to the establishment of a connection and the anticipation of seeing if it will germinate into something deeper; to the discovery of the animal allergies you do not have in common; to the first aesthetic or political disagreement the two of you have; to things either going somewhere or fizzling into thin air; to conversations about cohabitation; to rearrangements of closets and questions about the compatibility of long-term priorities and desires—every early stage of a relationship is a chance to witness the uncomfortable arising of your hopeful story lines, a chance to simply let them be by choosing to show up and see what happens next. It's probably a good idea to do a short mindfulness session before a date, to be aware of whatever story lines might be gripping your mind. It's okay to honor your story line, to bow to it, and then submit it gently for annihilation as you arrive at your date. The path to happiness always involves the death of a story line about what we think happiness means.

I will most likely kill your ideas about relationships in the morning.

Glimpsing that moment beyond hope and fear, you

might actually meet someone, if that's what you want. That part all depends on timing and circumstance. It is certainly possible. As you move through the dance of desire together, you might proclaim your own worthiness to this person, confidently: "With or without you, I am basically good." Then you might remember your innocence and get curious again: "But with you around, I have this hunch, life may get even *better.* Could we spend some time together and . . . just see what happens?"

The moment before you know how they'll respond is the most awakened moment of all.

As You Wish, Part I

The Practice of Partnership

> Mawidge is a dweam wiffin a dweam.
>
> —THE IMPRESSIVE CLERGYMAN

> Marriage is two people asking each other what
> they want for dinner until one of them dies.
>
> —INTERNET MEME

THE REAL BUTTERCUP'S NAME IS MARISSA. SHE HAS eyes like the sea after a storm.

In 2013, after those five years of dating and many more sojourns back and forth through the Kale Belt, I met my wife. The *Real Buttercup* is an ironic title, so ironic that its utterance resides on the same oxymoronic precipice that *relationship expert* inhabits. Eventually, though, enough irony can bend you back into reality, just as enough repetitions of dropping the story line can make you flexible enough to open up to the present moment. Sometimes when you stay open, something auspicious occurs, and you stumble across what works. Hence, beyond hope and fear, a Real Buttercup or Real Studmuffin may appear, and you may be wise enough to notice their arrival.

I didn't see her coming. Of course, we never see reality coming. That's how reality works, and how the relationship between ideas and direct experience works. When I met my wife in 2013, all the qualities from my earlier Buttercup list were still present, now appearing in a form unforeseen, an actuality beyond concept. She was not what my map had dictated, yet she was clearly what my desires had pointed me toward.

For millennia, Buddhist teachings on cognition have investigated the relationship between concepts and direct events. What is the link between an idea and an experience, between a map and a physical place? We attempt to prepare for reality by investing energy in concepts, images, and ideological lists. We have to do this in order to find our way in this world. These concepts can be helpful when they aren't stuck on a loop of obsession or perseveration. When we take the time to check our concepts against what we actually experience, they become great maps for navigating experience. Let's say you have a job interview coming up. Your preparation for the interview is an entirely conceptual act, necessarily so. If the interview is tomorrow (tomorrow is always a concept), it's good to have a résumé (concepts, hopefully not outright lies) and some image (concept) of what to wear, where to go (concept), who will be interviewing you (concept), what questions they might ask (concepts), and how you might craft your responses so they come across as perfectly spontaneous (spontaneity is often a concept pretending not to be one). But the moment you walk into the interview, even if you are well prepared and relaxed, you realize that your concepts had little to do with reality. The room, the person, the movements of your own body—suddenly all feel unanticipated. Preparing for life in the real world requires a conceptual map of the terrain ahead, just as the Buttercup list was my flawed, evolving map of what a good relationship might be. It's better to have clear concepts than flawed concepts. If you are spending the day in Chicago, it's better to follow a street map of Chicago rather than one of Toronto. But you can't spend the whole day looking at the map. Here's the most gorgeous feature of reality: it's *always* a surprise, even when experience dovetails with expectation. My wife was just that: a surprise.

The Real Buttercup and I had both been around the romantic block before, each of us seeing the annihilation of many personal story lines. Yet, when we met, we both experienced a moment of renewed innocence, a moment of *who are you?* as we tumbled down a steep hill together, once again very quickly. I am not sure who pushed whom. "Carpe Nowness," whispered the invisible forces of the universe, those energetic influences of which a skeptic will say, "I don't think they exist."

Meeting Marissa felt like a return to a native land. We did meet in the East Village. Yet something was fresh and new, familiar but undiscovered. Three qualities were different from my earlier Buttercup list.

First, kindness was much higher among our shared priorities, right below initial attraction. Kindness was the key to trusting each other so quickly. She was reliable, thoughtful, and diplomatic. Her friends, who were also kind (which is always an underestimated sign of someone you want to be around), told me you could set your watch to her, and I found out this was true. She sent thank-you cards; she contacted *my* friends and family on their birthdays. She kept people in mind, and she always followed through. These are not just social graces; these are mindfulness practices in and of themselves.

Second on the list was a sense of humor. I realized that if I was going to pursue a down-to-earth, spiritual path in this world of extreme beliefs, I needed someone who could bring humor to the journey. We deconstructed the cosmic jokes of our culture together, we cooked together, made fun of movies together, poked at the quirky ticks and odd vocabulary used in modern Buddhist lectures, especially mine. (Always beware the Buddhist who takes himself too seriously. The Real Buttercup consistently helps me avoid falling into that trap.)

Third, and most important, how we communicated in difficult times was brand-new. In the early days of our relationship, we had several significant arguments. Misunderstandings came strongly to the surface. We had arguments that reminded me of the pain of previous Fire Swamps, even the fires of my parents' relationship. We definitely didn't have the same expectations about how to communicate.

We spoke different languages. We both spoke English, yes, but our signals and gestures were not composed in the same idiom. I would love to say that there is some algebraic formula for loving communication. Indeed, there are many Buddhist tools for skillful listening and helpful speech in both peaceful and rough times.[1] Yet the crucial element was our coming back after arguments, each with a desire to learn from the other. That willingness to return, the same return that mindfulness is based on, was the part that felt new. It doesn't matter if you get off track, because you always will; coming back is the key to any successful practice.

After Marissa and I lived together for a year, before Christmas 2014, I composed and recited a mediocre poem for her on a public beach in Santa Monica, at sunset. Although many great poets have been meditators, sadly, mindfulness practice does nothing to increase the quality of your poetry. It only helps you stay present while you recite whatever poetry you happen to bring. Thankfully, the Real Buttercup was no tough crowd. I asked the question. She said yes.

The Power of a Vow

WE WERE MARRIED IN JUNE 2016. Our impressive clergywoman was Sharon Salzberg. She led us through an interactive ceremony in which we were invited to view ourselves as entering a commitment to practice together in relationship. Sharon kept mispronouncing "mawidge," but I didn't have the heart to correct her.

Are vows necessary? It's interesting to consider the purpose of marriage vows in modern times, beyond the cynical view that it's just about monetizing nostalgia. As a Buddhist teacher, I often get asked about the importance of taking vows. If the purpose of practice is to let go of story lines, then why would a Buddhist take a vow that leads to such a solid identification of husband and wife, or husband and husband, or wife and wife, or spouse and spouse? Why not just try to love each other the best you can without ruining the whole thing by proclaiming some bureaucratic identity? Why must the relationship be set in stone with ceremony and certificate? This is a similar question to one that I get asked regarding why we take a formal ceremonial vow to identify as Buddhist, or why we might eventually take a vow to follow a certain teacher, such as the vow I have taken with Sakyong Mipham Rinpoche. After all, you can live your life by whatever principles you choose, and you can commit to meditation without meeting some predetermined spiritual marker, a categorical signifier of membership to some club. In the same way, you could live with a partner for a long time, know you love each other, and never take any vow.

The ceremony of marriage, as best I can tell, continues to be such a cherished, and resented, aspect of our culture because it represents a witnessed celebration of two beings' commitment to practicing together. This committed practice includes all the practices of friendship, but also involves something more intimate, something more vulnerable, something more collaborative. The ritual of taking any vow involves overcoming our early mammalian need to run when things get the least bit sticky or claustrophobic. A vow of marriage, just like a formal vow of commitment to a spiritual path, is a way to tell your sweet little amygdala, "I see you, old friend, you terrified baby salamander, you timid little squirrel. I know you want to run and hide sometimes, I know you often need to be reactive in order to feel safe, but you've taken this vow now, and this vow is a reminder to just come back. You are learning to stay or, more realistically, to come back whenever you begin to run. You vow to come back, to work with all the tenderness and discomfort and uncertainty. You got dressed up, even wore a pocket square and boutonniere, and all your friends cleaned up so nice for the occasion. Why not practice leaning in and staying when times are tough?" Leaning in is the only way awakening occurs.

Sharon spoke of the practice of kindness, and then our friends and family took turns with the practice of marriage based on a series of relational practices called the *paramitas*, or ways of transcending confusion when working with others. Like everything else, marriage is a practice. If you lose sight of seeing it as a practice, you will suffer. If you keep this view in sight, you will probably still suffer, but at least you will use the opportunity of your joint suffering to open up rather than shut down.

The Practice of Partnership

A COMMITTED PARTNERSHIP IS WHAT happens after the credits roll in *The Princess Bride* (and in most rom-coms in history). Day-by-day commitment is the hardest part of any story to convey, because most of what we live through in relationships is mundane, repetitive, and without climax.[2] First, every practice that applies to friendship applies to marriage. If you don't establish a basis of friendship first, you're probably not going to last as a couple. Marriage is a constant practice of trust, inspiration, and letting go—and of conquering inner villains. But marriage is something more than friendship, because it is a practice that leads back to the very roots of working with the dance of desire, over a much longer arc of time than just a few dates or a casual relationship. To work with wisdom over a long period of time, you might make use of the following principles and practices.

Cool Boredom:
Realizing That Nothing Really Happens

ONE OF THE GREATEST BENEFITS of meditation is also one of its most unmarketable. In my tradition, this profound experience has an unprofound name: *cool boredom.* Your relationship with boredom, with the irritation you feel when not much new or noteworthy is happening, is one of the most important aspects of developing emotional maturity. Boredom is also one of the most important practices we can have if our planet is going to survive the consumerism that is currently decimating the environment. Life is full of many wonders, yet each moment of adult life is fairly familiar and routine. In a sense, meditation reveals to you a very discomforting truth: most of the time, *nothing* is happening, at least not anything newsworthy. If you want some wow factor, you usually have to construct a derivative "wow" out of the scraps of previous experiences. The taste of coffee is nothing new. The accelerating pace of each news cycle tends toward a recycling of previously reported dramas. The blockbuster movies you look forward to seeing you've already seen when they were called something else. The music we listen to samples or covers the hits of the past. The very book you are reading right now is just a new take on old material, which is itself a new take on old material. And in meditation, you realize that the thoughts you think seem to be pointing to the cyclical sameness of adult life, that redundancy, a boring recurrence called "me."

Cool boredom is preceded by something more irritating, more destabilizing, more anxiety-producing—something called *hot boredom*. Our inability to rest our minds when not much is happening is one of our greatest weaknesses. Our whole world seems caught in FOMO, the "fear of missing out," the pretense that something crucial might be happening someplace else and we just didn't get the secret invite. We often get bored in meditation because we believe that the technique of mindfulness is not in itself profound enough. Maybe mindfulness is causing us to miss another "now" elsewhere, a now that is somehow more refined, riper, bursting with more flavor and profundity.

In meditation, discipline is about staying with the irritation of hot boredom. Eventually, when you trust the redundancy of the technique, your fight-or-flight response settles down. Subsequently, you become less reactive. In the space where reactions used to take charge, appreciation now grows. You start to consider what is already happening, like discovering a treasure hidden right under your nose. When you slow down, the exact same coffee tastes better, the brick and trees and grass and graffiti look more interesting. As your boredom cools off, there is even a tiny bit of space in between your thoughts. This is the space of mobility that allows creative insight to occur. And when you slow down further into cool boredom, you realize that you neither need to consume nor construct experiences in order to be happy. In the space of cool boredom, the ordinary becomes magical, the redundant becomes refreshed, and longevity becomes sustainable.

A committed relationship is a practice of boredom, mixed with the dance of desire. It includes tremendous familiarity and mundane repetition. It is a practice with the same person day in and day out. *Cool boredom* is a great phrase to describe how you have to practice after the curtain falls on your courtship, so to speak. Relationships can also be viewed as a shared meditation practice. If you don't have the ability to appreciate each other when there isn't a huge plot moment, you probably aren't going to last long. In meditation, you get to practice cool boredom with yourself. In a relationship, you get to practice it even more powerfully with another person. The only way to discover cool boredom is to stay present, through the gauntlet of fight or flight, holding your mind through the irritation that always accompanies repetition, the simple rituals of relating.

Finding freshness in the repetitive perceptions of daily life is the key to uncovering wisdom.

I admit, I really like getting bored with the Real Marissa.

Patience:
Fighting the Basically Good Fight

IT IS NEVER FUN TO argue. Some people claim that they *like* fighting, but I don't believe them. I think some people like the possibility of "winning" an argument, but in a committed relationship, nobody wins. We could say that this is true in any human relationship, that every argument is fought without a victor, given that we are tasked with increasing our ability to care about the well-being of all beings. The truth that nobody wins an argument is especially obvious in a committed partnership, because if one person ends up miserable, feeling unheard and disrespected, you can bet that it will soon end up being the other person's problem as well. A committed relationship tends to be as happy as its least satisfied member. On the other hand, whenever I hear a couple say they never argue, I get nervous. Like everything else, there is a middle path to arguing, and the argument itself is both a practice and a manifestation of basic goodness. To assume that there is the possibility of relationship without disagreement is, once again, to misunderstand the dance of desire.

Disagreement is embedded in the truth of attraction. Again, all romantic relationships arise because something called "me" longs to connect with something that is "other." This sounds great, expansive, magnetic. But then you realize that what initially attracted you to the other, their unique perspective and all those qualities that you don't possess, also means that, well, they have a *different* perspective on things.

"Other's" mother didn't raise her the way "my" mother raised me. "Other" has different aesthetic preferences, and a different hierarchy of needs determines her methodology for arranging both refrigerator and kitchen cabinets. "Other" plays loud workout music while "me" tries to meditate, then "other" tries to meditate while "me" practices yoga and listens to (objectively, obviously) cooler music. "Other" gets understandably restless after she's heard all of "me's" jokes a few times, which weren't that great to begin with. "Me" and "other" are primed by the nature of subjectivity to occasionally disagree. Of course, every couple has to decide which large-scale disagreements signify incompatibility and which are workable. But even "workable" differences are guaranteed to be significant, because that is, quite literally, what it means to commit to an "other" person. That's why you were attracted to them in the first place. The practice of patience is not about quelling disagreement, but about accommodating, leaving space for the inevitable divergences in a relationship. Patience is far easier to practice if you accept the truth that you are supposed to disagree sometimes. Such is the nature of subjectivity and attraction, self and other.

Traditionally, practicing patience, also translated as forbearance, is about skillfully navigating anger and aggression, both when we are feeling anger ourselves and when we are on the receiving end of someone else's irritation. Patience views anger as a teachable moment, and realizes that at the root of the anger is always a being who is in pain. Patience transforms the energy of hatred into a harmonizing, or at least a comprehending, of different points of view.

Of course, even to attempt to understand another person's perspective, you need to be able to trust that they have nonmanipulative intentions, that they are arguing in good faith, which is why the rules of friendship still apply in romantic partnership. Patience, as both inherent quality and a mental muscle that strengthens with practice, is the aspect of your mind that isn't so surprised or insulted by the inevitability of disagreement. Patience looks forward to some level of disharmony as an opportunity to get to work, rather than viewing an argument as some failure of your equanimity.

This kind of accommodation and forbearance is hard enough to practice with a stranger or casual acquaintance, a situation where there isn't much at stake (*no, please, please, you go, you were here first*) but with an intimate partner, the practice is more intense. When a partnership is involved, there is much more depth of identity, as well as threats to that identity. Luckily, the vow of patience in a committed relationship allows you to argue without needing to resolve each argument perfectly. If you are committed to another person and they are committed to you, you can learn that not every trigger needs to be acted upon immediately. When you don't feel trusted or safe, you can lose sight of this and fall back into a need for instant expression and immediate resolution. There is no better practice than arguing with your partner to see that self and other both hold valid perspectives, and to see that most of the things that piss you off are momentary irritants that, when expressed and worked with over time, can often be healed fairly easily. The point of an argument is not to adopt another person's point of view; it's to accept its existence and move forward from there.

Westley comes back to life with the help of a truly exemplary, and truly strange, long-term couple. Max and Valerie have clearly mastered some of the practices related to durability in a relationship. In particular, they seem to have the practice of patience down. Applauding their relationship may seem a strange thing to do. They yell at each other: he calls her a witch, she calls him a liar. They could probably learn a thing or two about Buddhist teachings on mindful listening and kind speech, for sure.

But the real miracle of Max and Valerie is that they have made their way into old age together, and they can speak difficult truths to each other at the right moment. It must have something to do with knowing how to argue, how to be direct, when to point out the other's insecurities and self-deceptions, and how not to view the other's insights as a threat. "Have fun storming the castle," they are finally able to say to the posse of young crusaders, full of sudden joy, because they have already found their place, and arguing is just a part of life for them. In classic Buddhism, appropriate listening and kind speech are traditional practices that carry guidelines for avoiding harshness, divisive gossip, and speaking mistruths. Still, right speech is a practice that comes to life when a relationship develops its own cadence and language. Every relationship has its own language. I don't talk to my best friends the same way I talk to a meditation student. What might be a hilarious joke in one relationship is an insult in another, and a basically good argument utilizes the language that has been agreed upon by its participants, as long as they have indeed agreed. Who am I to judge Max and Valerie's way of speaking to each other? They've been at it a lot longer than I have, and it works for them.

Joyous Effort

I IMAGINE THAT AFTER THE film ends, Max and Valerie go on a date together, trying to discover a great MLT restaurant they haven't checked out yet. During our marriage ceremony, as family and friends offered their modern interpretations and symbolic gifts representing various Buddhist relationship practices, our friend Eleanor gave us a Rubik's Cube to represent committing to the relational practice of joyous effort, also called exertion. The Rubik's Cube is something youthful, playful, colorful, engaging, and very difficult to solve. In spiritual practice, joyous effort relates to recovering your inner energy and inspiration, but not necessarily to solve a puzzle. Instead, the effort is about regaining your interest in the game all over again. Joyous effort helps you recover your *prana*, regroup and refresh your intent, or discover new momentum whenever you feel depleted or overwhelmed.

The effort of rediscovery is the flip side of working with cool boredom. When you truly see that you can't make anything "new" happen, you realize that you need some re-inspired effort to recover your relation to the events of the world, and your relationship to the person you've formerly known as an object of attraction.

At first it may seem that joyous effort in "Buddhist" relationships is about turning "me" and "other" into a singular entity called "we," living safely within the peacefulness of that supposed unity. In many ways, there is a trustworthy melding that happens in a committed relationship. But while harmony and deep connection might be found, "oneness" is never achievable. Interestingly, there is no such thing as oneness in Buddhism. It's not a Buddhist term, and not the same thing as interdependence. Sometimes the mysterious expression "not one, and not two" is employed within Middle Way philosophy to describe the nuances of interdependence between two beings. Two beings are not "one" because they each have distinct minds, perspectives, and longings. But they are also not separate from each other, because they affect each other constantly, so a couple is not quite "two," in a sense of total separation. All beings are interconnected, but we remain distinct entities within the realm of the mind.

I am never going to completely know my wife, and part of her should remain a mystery. From the standpoint of certainty, this may seem terrifying, but from the standpoint of relationship longevity and awakening, a fresh mystery is always necessary, even if you know your partner well. Thankfully, the "other" never completely joins with "me," so the perpetual dance of desire waits to be rediscovered and reinterpreted, just like inspiration for meditation practice needs to be occasionally refreshed, especially when the practice stagnates or grows distant from you.

Just because nothing profoundly new is happening, that doesn't mean we can't help each other experience life from a fresh perspective. There's an obvious need to keep investing in new hobbies, new sexuality, new voyages. We do this not to solve a Rubik's Cube or find permanent solutions, but to feel the rewards of effort itself, the reward of the "other's" rediscovery. In Buddhist thought, if you find the right balance of effort, mixing a relaxed attitude with the work it takes to show up, effort actually *increases* your energy rather than depleting it. If your efforts increase your energy, you know you are working in the right direction. (That Rubik's Cube sits in front of me as I write this.)

I know romantic partnership is not for every human. If my personal journey or my examples appear too male-oriented, too heteronormatively bourgeois, too partner-centric, too Buddhist or Buddh-ish, then please accept my apology. When it comes to romance and desire, to each their own. I do know that the dance of desire and deep connections to other beings are both part of the path of awakening. Desire and love are universal truths, inseparable from inhabiting a human body. If you learn how to appreciate the dance in intimate relationships, you might just be prepared for the deepest battleground of any human journey: the struggle with your own lineage, the dharma of family.

PART III

THE DHARMA OF FAMILY

It's possible you could become enlightened
everywhere *except* with your family.

—CHÖGYAM TRUNGPA RINPOCHE

All Sentient Beings
Have Been Grandpa

Grandson: Grandpa, you read that wrong! . . .
It wouldn't be fair.
Grandpa: Who said life was fair? Where is that
written?

INSTANTLY AND FOREVER, THE MOMENT HE ARRIVES
on-screen, Peter Falk will remind me of Grandpa Sol.

There is a moment you recognize, intuitively and viscerally, that the stories we tell each other are always just the
story within the story. The real story has to do with the
people who pass their stories along. The real story happens
when you observe a tale's transmission. This act of passing

narratives down across generations is what creates a human lineage. *The Princess Bride* knows this, so it includes within its plot, like food served in an edible package, the story's telling, an encounter between a grandfather and his grandson on a sick day home from school in the "real" world. Director Rob Reiner agreed that this relationship was the purpose of the entire movie.

The story that became the book that became the movie was created by William Goldman, a bedtime "as you wish" for his two young daughters. One daughter wanted a story about a princess; the other wanted a story about a bride—hence the title. Even in the book version, Goldman insists on not being perceived as the author, instead crediting "S. Morgenstern." Also, he claims to have been read the story himself by his father, and asserts he has chosen to relay to the reader only the "good parts."[1]

Thus, the most crucial interaction of *The Princess Bride*—the relationship between grandfather and grandson—is the one that receives by far the least screen time. Every single time the real story begins, every single time Peter Falk arrives on-screen somewhere in Evanston, Illinois, to visit his grandson, I think of Grandpa Sol visiting me, when I was almost exactly the same age as the Grandson, in Manhattan. As I have been grandfatherless for the last twenty-nine years of loving this movie, you will forgive me for visualizing Peter Falk entering my bedroom and telling me some kind of story, any kind of story.

By June 1988, at the end of fourth grade, I had lost all my own grandfathers and was just beginning my love affair with *The Princess Bride*. (I think I had seen it only once or twice by then.) That's right. I said "all my own grand-fathers." Depending on the strictness of your accounting method, I have had either two or three grandfathers. My mother's father, a fairly legendary patriarch in small-town Arkansas, died the year before I was born. Everybody says we would've gotten along famously, if only the space-time continuum could fold like origami paper to bring us to-gether as grown men. I imagine him as some supporting character in a Faulkner novel.

Second, my father always says that Chögyam Trungpa (who died the previous spring of 1987, at the tender age of forty-seven) was a spiritual father to him. This would make him a sort of spiritual grandfather to me. I met Trungpa Rinpoche a variety of times as a young boy but don't have many strong memories of him, other than of his general kind presence. It was truly impressive how a partially par-alyzed Tibetan man donning a three-piece suit could speak confidently, in a mildly effeminate British accent, no less, while hundreds of Westerners waited upon his every word.

At Trungpa Rinpoche's cremation ceremony on an un-seasonably hot day in the Northeast Kingdom of Vermont in early June 1987, the assembled adults were somber. Their loss was palpable and hovering. I didn't recognize it then, but I was watching several thousand grown-ups grieving a hybrid of best friend, father, and guru. They'd all lost him before anyone was ready to let go, even though that was exactly what their Buddhist practices had trained them to do. But we children were oddly playful, almost celebratory, unsure how to properly arrange our behavior for the spiri-tual bon voyage of our parents' unlikely Tibetan hero. Most of us had no rule book for how to *be* at the cremation of a Tibetan lama. For us kids, the ceremony almost felt like a picnic. When multiple rainbows and seemingly supernatural cloud formations appeared during the day's events, it felt perfectly normal.

Perhaps calling Chögyam Trungpa a grandfather is too poetic, an unlicensed stretch, but there is something about the figures who receded before you came of age that hold the same place a grandparent holds, that mysterious archive beneath a trap door, that treasure chest of wisdom waiting to be unlocked through the transmission of stories that come to you little by little as you age, the collected insights of a life whose glory years ended before your own prime began.

With those two already gone by 1988, Grandpa Sol remained the only grandfather I knew well, the one whose bushy eyebrows and musky grandpa scent fill my awareness whenever Peter Falk enters his disinterested and spoiled grandson's bedroom in *The Princess Bride* to read Morgenstern's fairy tale.

A few days before the end of the fourth grade, I came home from school to my early childhood apartment on the Upper West Side of Manhattan. I don't have many fond memories of that place during this period, but it's not the apartment's fault. It was the sort of apartment on which New York real estate legends of the 1970s and '80s are based: a prewar rent-stabilized fortress. Shadowy and sprawling, it was the kind of residence you cannot find in Manhattan anymore without being a multimillionaire. But the place was emotionally darkened by the long-coming collapse of

my parents' marriage. (Two months later, they would finally separate for good, ironically enough, while we were
staying at the home of Christopher Guest's parents.) This
afternoon may be the last memory I have of my parents together. My afternoon hours were usually a lull, a hidden
space after the drudgery of another day at fourth grade as a
nerdy outcast, before the pain of homebound evenings bear-
ing witness to another of my very Buddhist parents'
seemingly very "un-Buddhist" arguments. I was an only
child, without any siblings to absorb the impact of their war
of attrition. My afternoons were a private limbo in which to
hide, when I'd flee into either Riverside Park or my bedroom.

Today was different, though. Everybody was home early,
sitting in the living room, the furniture washed in the pre-
solstice light of early June. There were Mom, Dad, and a
mysterious guest who *never* came to our apartment: Grandpa
Sol. I saw Grandpa Sol at least once a week, but we would
always bring ourselves to the apartment he shared with his
second wife, Edith, across Manhattan, most often for Sunday brunch. We normally went to him because his mobility
was compromised. He was only sixty-eight, but his advancing
Parkinson's disease left him hobbled. Now he was here, on
our couch, smiling a fluid smile under his thick eyebrows,
having made the journey across the island on a random
weekday afternoon, sitting pleasantly with both my parents.
The idea of both my parents being home simultaneously, facing each other and smiling, was one huge surprise. Grandpa
Sol's presence was a whole 'nother level of happy coincidence. I brightened quickly.

We all walked to the park together, and I didn't mind

how slowly the usually three-minute journey to the playground unfolded today. Grandpa moved uneasily, his arms caught in tremors at his sides, as if he were trapped inside a looping GIF image, the individual frames of his movement muted by pain. When we got to the park, Grandpa Sol didn't read me any fairy tales; I think we just sat on a bench together. In earlier days, when Grandpa's illness was less an obstacle, he would tell me a story, or help me cheat and find the hidden *afikomen* matzo at his Passover seders before any of the other kids, who were not his bloodline, could make the discovery and pawn their unleavened bread for cash. I felt both honored by and ashamed of his spiritual nepotism.

On the bench, he asked about my summer plans. I shrugged as I spoke, unexcited about the time ahead. Grandpa didn't return my dissatisfied frown. Instead, he smiled. He must have known that things were going to get better for me. He wasn't clairvoyant, but he had what all grandparents have: the context of life's full arc. So he knew that impermanence always has a plus side: he knew that fourth grade would end in a few days, and fifth grade would begin. And when the fall arrived, things would indeed improve for me. In fifth grade, a new best friend would emerge. The wounds from my two surgeries would finish healing. I would get used to living in two households, and would even find a sense of freedom in the weekly back-and-forth across the city. Grandpa Sol did not look worried about me at all.

I'm pretty sure we both said "I love you" when he left. I'm sure I said it the way we humans too often say "I love you," as if the syllables and the inconceivable devotion they signify are just passing each other in a gaggle of distracted thoughts. I'm pretty sure I forgot to ask Dad why Grandpa had come to our apartment anyway, even though I instinctively knew that the surprise visit wasn't something I should get used to. The whole afternoon was a mini fairy tale, set in a vanishing kingdom called Nichtern.

A few days later, my father came into my room to tell me that Grandpa Sol and Edith, my stepgrandmother, had died together in their apartment. I don't believe he used the exact word when he told me they were gone, but no one hid the fact that their death had been a double suicide. I remember even then feeling some understanding about why they had done it. To this day, their deaths make considerably more sense to me than Trungpa Rinpoche's did the year before. The *New York Times* obituary page recorded their deaths publicly as suicide, the result of a calculated overdose of sleeping pills. Later I learned that Sol and Edith's weekly cleaning lady had discovered them Monday, about thirty-six hours after their passing. They had put on their finest, she in an evening dress and he in a suit, and had a wonderful last Saturday-night date together in their apartment. The cleaning lady discovered them in their bed, dressed to the nines, a sexagenarian Romeo with a septuagenarian Juliet. I have always imagined them spooning each other as their breaths finally ceased, but who knows?

Grandpa Sol had engaged his own existential calculus, within his own understanding of the truth of suffering, deciding that the pain of his condition was too great to justify going on. His slightly older, but healthier wife, Edith, in the ultimate "as you wish" gesture, had decided to go with him. In preparation, Grandpa had spent the final week of his life surprise-visiting everybody who was important to him (without revealing his intentions). And that was why he had come to us that afternoon, instead of our going to see him.

Perhaps more than any physical disintegration, the nature of memory itself is the greatest exploration of impermanence we can undertake. According to neuroscience, each explicit memory is far less solidly etched than we believe. Each time we recall an old memory, we re-encode it based on current circumstances, mood, and environment. As Dr. Daniel Siegel says, "Memory is not a static thing, but an active set of processes. Even the most 'concrete' experiences . . . are actually dynamic representational processes."[2] Each time we actively consider an explicit memory, we rewrite the file. Each time we recollect a moment, we are tracing our way further from the light, sound, and textural perceptions of the actual event in question. It's like each memory is a Xerox of a Xerox of a Xerox, a reprint which we then use like a coloring book, and then copy again. Each time we remember, we are not remembering the moment in question. The moment in question is gone. We are simply remembering the last time we recalled the moment, the environment and attitude we experienced during its previous recollections.

It's probable that my memory of the last time Grandpa Sol came to visit is a file corrupted by Hollywood, altered each and every time I've seen *The Princess Bride*. It is possible that each viewing of the film rewrites and reshapes the memory of my own grandpa, making the Dr. Sol Nichtern

I know far more story line than story. Regardless, I was more or less the same age as Fred Savage's grandson character. And that's probably why every time I see Peter Falk come on-screen, I instantly think of Grandpa Sol. And then I think of the importance of lineage, and the importance of understanding family as a spiritual practice.

Making Family Your Practice

CHÖGYAM TRUNGPA USED TO SAY it's possible you could become enlightened everywhere except around your family. In other words, the family is perhaps the very last frontier of awakening, occurring *after* one has developed a healthy connection with oneself, with friends, with partnership, with work, and maybe with everyone else. With this statement in mind, it's easier to see why so many practitioners look to leave the world behind. Never mind the difficulty of other people; maybe it was *family* that the great masters left society in order to escape. Given his relationship with his overbearing and narcissistic father, Siddhartha Gautama is one practitioner to whom this premise might readily apply.

If what Chögyam Trungpa Rinpoche said is true, then the converse of his statement is also true: if your relationship with family becomes more awake and compassionate, you will have the skills necessary to awaken any other kind of relationship. If you can become enlightened around your family, awakening elsewhere will be a piece of cake.

And if you can look to all people, perhaps all beings, as members of a family with whom you are in the process of healing, then enlightened society would be easy to achieve.

If family becomes part of your practice, it becomes much easier to engage in the irritations and disagreements of a larger society. Many of the political disagreements that dominate our world seem to stem from differing definitions of family: who gets included, who gets excluded, and how a family should be arranged in terms of patriarchy and matriarchy, competition and collaboration, structure and freedom, obedience and dissent. It's possible that if we start to acknowledge the wisdom of our family lineages, we might be able to expand our definition of family to include more and more people. In the end, the human race is merely a family whose members are removed from one another by degrees of separation that are far more theoretical than biological.

The seed of the political struggles of society are often planted with those closest to us. Part of the difficulty in practicing with your own family is this: it is often hard to tell whose karma is whose. Let's imagine that a very confused or even mentally ill person approaches you on the street and begins yelling at you, telling you that something you had no direct part in, like 9/11 or Pearl Harbor, was all your fault. Maybe you would be scared for your safety, but you would at least know that the other person had their own stuff going on. You might be startled, but you wouldn't take the attack personally or begin to question your role in Pearl Harbor. After you ensured your safety, you might even be able to send the person accosting you a compassionate wish, because you would see their confusion and know that you were not to blame, at least not personally, for the difficult internal experience they are having. Within the realm of mental reactions, when you know what is yours and what is someone else's, it makes it easier to help another human being, because you no longer take their confusion so personally.

Similarly, it's an interesting exercise to spend time with the family of someone you know, witnessing their interactions as a friendly outsider. Perhaps you see the family members getting on each other's nerves, their mixed reactions such as anger or defensiveness, which seem to happen a little bit more quickly than might be called for, at least from your third-party position. From your perch of relative objectivity, it's easier to see when someone is caught up in their habitual patterns. You might even find the minor irritations of that family, that family that is not yours, adorable and endearing.

Now, let's say that during Thanksgiving with your own family, an argument breaks out at the dinner table, an argument about your family's own Pearl Harbor moments. Suddenly it is much harder to tell who is reacting, who is projecting onto whom. *Am I the crazy person here? Are you the crazy one? Are we all crazy?* In families, triggers and projections enmesh, and the jumbled wires of habitual perception often become nearly impossible to disentangle.

Something happens within a family, a kind of karmic claustrophobia, a hybrid of true love and tangled irritation.

Sometimes it's even hard for mindfulness to operate in the realm of family, much less for compassion to swoop in and save the day. Mindfulness is based on a simple but difficult premise: that you can directly witness what is arising in your own mind. Mindfulness presupposes that, upon reflection, you can note your reactivity to a sense perception or impulse, either during its immediate arising or after the fact.

This is why we often formally practice mindfulness on the meditation cushion. A practice session is sort of like a flight simulator. It's a way to slow down the pace of external stimuli so that you can witness a perception, and feel your reactions to that perception. But in life, especially around family, mindfulness becomes far more difficult. This isn't just due to the increased pace of stimuli. The problem is that your own reactivity becomes enmeshed with the reactivity of those family members around you. In family, due to karmic entanglements, shared biology, shared attachments, and shared experiences from a very young age, it becomes harder to clarify what is arising in your own mind and what is arising in someone else's. It's very hard to say whose reaction is whose, which karma is which. Sometimes it's hard to tell which *mind* is which, or which thoughts are spoken by which voice.

It's always helpful to step back and remember your intention to be kind to yourself and to others before jumping into the fray and spending time around members of your family. Many meditation techniques, especially those that focus on a compassionate intention in relationships, help you to step back and create such an intention.

Meditation on Relationships
and the Benefactor

WITHIN THE TEACHINGS OF SHAMBHALA Buddhism, there is a wide variety of methods for delivering into your practice a healthier and friendlier connection with relationships, both in formal meditation and in every aspect of life. These include practices like loving-kindness meditation, *tonglen* (sending and receiving compassion meditation), visualization (the imaginative practice of visualizing superheroes of compassion, called bodhisattvas and *yidams*), and meditations on forgiveness and healing, both for oneself and for those you are in conflict with or feel wronged by.

In these meditations, you often first choose a figure from your own lineage, somebody who embodies safety, love, and wisdom. This chosen figure is generally called the "benefactor." Your benefactor could be a hero, a teacher, or an elder. In *The Princess Bride*, the benefactor is precisely what the Grandfather represents to the Grandson: wisdom, strength, and unconditional love (plus much unacknowledged patience) on a sick day. In these various relationship meditations, you might first visualize this benefactor's presence in front of you. You can even imagine that they are offering you the direction you need in order to open your heart to yourself and others.

In the various compassion and visualization techniques I've practiced, many beings have appeared as benefactor: my grandparents, my guru Sakyong Mipham, personal teachers and mentors such as Sharon Salzberg and Dr. Gaylon Ferguson, social heroes like Dr. Martin Luther King Jr., creative heroes such as Allen Ginsberg, childhood heroes like Fezzik and Papa Smurf (welcome to my mind), and Buddhist bodhisattvas such as Tara, the archetype of compassionate and relentless action on behalf of others. More often than not, the particular meditation technique dictates which sort of benefactor you choose to imagine. In some practices, such as loving-kindness meditation, you can spontaneously choose your own benefactor at the beginning of a given session, based on whomever comes to mind.

The benefactor's role in these meditations is simple: in order to allow your system to generate love, you have to feel love yourself. It's that simple. You can't bake bread unless you know what bread is, and you can't generate compassion without feeling the positive transference of a few droplets of care onto yourself. Ancient Buddhist teachers understood implicitly, even without the theory of mirror neurons, that our minds reflect the behavior of others, and that when we imagine being supported by beings who already manifest the experience of compassion, it becomes easier to recall this quality, and eventually to embody it. Finally, we can offer love to others.

A classical Tibetan contemplation on compassion asks the meditator to consider the implications of the primary benefactor within one's life. The contemplation takes the form of the phrase "All sentient beings have been my mother" and is based on the idea that each of our "mindstreams" proceeds through many iterations and across an unlimited period of time in which sentient beings have existed and will exist. Therefore, we each have experienced and will experience an infinite number of intimate relationships, an unlimited number of mothers. Any truth contained in this phrase is based on your ability to expand your notion of space and time beyond the confinements of just one life cycle, beyond one particular group of relationships, beyond one way of relating to the characters currently populating your own life.

This contemplation is based on belief in reincarnation, but more important, it is based on the compelling vision of a universe with far more sentient relationships than we can imagine when we are caught up in temporary dramas. The Tibetan contemplation is a kind of emotional yoga asana, a stretch toward a feeling of greater inclusivity. In the longest possible view of time, we will crisscross again with the beings we meet in some shape and form. We have already crossed paths with those we meet, depending on them as a helpless child looks to a nurturing parent. "All sentient beings have been my mother" is a gorgeous invitation to expansiveness, whether or not it contains scientific truth. Western theorists have wondered how a child might attain a secure attachment to its mother, but ancient Tibetans wondered how a person might eventually develop a secure attachment to *everyone*. Like much of the philosophy based on mindfulness, this contemplation moves us beyond the puppetry of our hyperreactive limbic systems. This contemplation helps us see that the roles people play in our personal universe can and will switch: a threatening adversary can become beloved, given the right time and circumstances.

Anyone who has ever gone through a difficult breakup

knows the phenomenon of sudden categorical switches, that disjointed moment your heart's regard for your lover flips from "for me" to "against me." In separation, your former favorite person gets re-identified, often as a tyrant, overnight. This is why conflict is so painful: because it causes you to distrust that you can be certain about the way you have categorized others. *Was I wrong to ever love that person? Am I wrong to love the people I love now?* How would you treat this person who is angering you right now if you knew, at another time and place in karmic history, that person had been your mother and sacrificed all to care for you when you were helpless?

Of course, contemplating one's mother can bring up tremendously complex feelings. It has been argued that this emotional complexity is a phenomenon of the Western world, and that in ancient Tibet, people generally had simpler, more unconditionally loving feelings toward their mothers. So, in Tibet, when you were instructed to open your mind to the vast possibilities of connection in the statement "All sentient beings have been my mother," these words helped you soften your heart, enabling you to relax into the securest sense of attachment and the deepest sense of connection. The thought of your mother, Tibetans said, reminded you of your own vulnerability, opening you up to the tenderness of love, and that love could be transposed onto the person you were having problems with at the moment. If each practitioner could map the memory of the tenderness your mother showed you onto your obstacle-ridden relationships, the logic went, then you could deal more effectively with the difficulty in front of you.

I have no ability to discern whether ancient Tibetans actually experienced more secure attachment to their primary caregivers than Westerners do. However, for many people I know, mothers are the ones we have the *hardest* time with, so this contemplation might strike an unintended chord. If you had an absent or abusive mother and then were instructed to contemplate "All sentient beings have been my mother," who knows what that might bring up for you? And what if you were using the contemplation to try to develop compassion for a difficult person such as Donald Trump? "You want me to imagine Trump magically appearing in my imagination as my neurotic mother?" The jumbled visualization that might follow could bring up a maelstrom of rough feelings, to say the least.

My teacher Sakyong Mipham updated the phrasing of this contemplation to consider all beings as having been one's "personal protector," a designation that doesn't require you to think about a specific, and possibly very painful, person in your lineage. Instead, you get to imagine a benefactor of your choosing. When you recall them, their presence offers you that sense of protection, a feeling of belonging, knowing that things are fundamentally workable. This kind of secure attachment is what, in an enlightened society, we might get from family relations and especially from our parental figures—a confidence that propels us into the world with compassion and open-mindedness.

What if we included our grandparents in this contemplation? "All sentient beings have been my grandfather/grandmother." For me, even in grief and absence, the contemplation of my grandparents has created a sense of genuine heart opening, a feeling of being loved and trusted to carry a lineage forward. For the sick and confused Grandson in *The Princess Bride*, the grandparent is personal protector, benefactor, and model of safety, a way of remembering that his lineage can be seen as a welcome harbor instead of the original problem in his universe.

My advice for preparing to practice with family is simple: take it slow. Without a doubt, there is a lot to work with that is painful, and many rich experiences to harvest. As is the case with friends and lovers, it won't make sense to be in an active relationship with certain family members. But you may still make those people part of your loving-kindness practice. First, though, it might serve you to contemplate and acknowledge your own place in your family history.

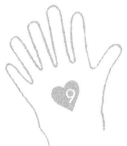

Fred Savage Is a Jerk, and I Am Fred Savage

Gratitude for Your Lineage

> If you had a roommate that did any of the things babies do, you'd ask them to move out.
>
> —JIM GAFFIGAN

I REMEMBER TELLING A FRIEND, A MOTHER OF A young child, about my idea to write this book.

"Oh, I get it," she said. "It's like what would happen if Fred Savage's character grew up to teach Buddhism."

At first, I bristled at the comparison. "Well, okay. Sure. Except the Grandson is a complete jerk to his Grandfather in the movie. And to his mom."

"Aren't we all, though?" my friend said. "I mean, seriously, every kid is a jerk. They have no idea what we sacrifice for them. My son is an asshole to me, maybe ... let's say eighty percent of the time. He's pretty much the worst roommate in the world."

Precious Human Life

WHAT IS YOUR OWN PLACE among your relatives? When you consider your role as a member of your family lineage, does the thought of where you come from invoke resentment, fear, apathy, and sadness, or pride, gratitude, and appreciation? Maybe all the above? Hopefully, our basic experience of family is an even deeper version of the great qualities of friendship. In an ideal world, family is where we go to regenerate trust in our basic goodness. But what if you have certain family relationships that don't work that way? And what if, like many, you've experienced conflict or trauma, or are estranged from members of your family?

Perhaps it is best to begin with gratitude. The issue many of us face with any practice of gratitude is how forced, how fake it often seems, like giving or receiving a compliment you know isn't sincere. But we aren't talking about fake compliments. Like every other practice, gratitude can be viewed as a mental muscle for positivity, a form of contemplative struggle that it's worthwhile to pursue. Even if your family history is difficult, you can practice offering gratitude for the sacrifices your lineage has made on your behalf, and the positive experiences passed along.

Modern science demonstrates why gratitude is such a crucial element of human experience. We often feel incredibly negative about the legacy of being born human. For many, this negativity is justified, arising from a social inheritance that includes poverty, racism, sexism, and trauma. But for just a moment, let's say, you are a relatively privileged member of this society, like the Grandson in *The Princess Bride*. We each carry a spoiled child around inside, and the spoiled child often makes a prominent appearance, especially during the struggles of meditation practice. The spoiled kid in each of us just doesn't want to deal with any of it right now: not with growing up, not with work; not with relationships and family, aging, illness, or the letdowns of daily life; and definitely not with the mind itself. To my inner spoiled child, even a delayed train or dreary weather is rich material for complaints about life in general. Like the Grandson, and like me much of the time in fourth grade, we would love to call in sick to life.

The grouchy kid in me grows more spoiled when it comes to the details of family. That inner fourth-grader tends to view family obligations as a hardship. Where does all this negativity about family come from? It comes first from our evolution, and the corrective mechanism is the contemplation of gratitude. Gratitude might be more necessary now than ever. As Suzanne C. Parker of American University states, "The modern, Western-centric value of maintaining independence can lead to a tendency to idolize self-reliance, prize uniqueness, and perceive differences rather than similarities, eroding a felt sense of interdependence and gratitude." Ancient Buddhist teachers lacked the physical precision of modern brain science, but they implicitly understood the psychological need for gratitude. From the subjective science of their own experience, they saw that we enter this human life with a bias toward negativity. This bias can be amplified based on difficult circumstances that happen within the early dynamics of families.

Because our nervous systems are geared toward spotting threats to survival in the highly predatory environment of the ancient world (snakes, saber-toothed tigers, and natural disasters of unusual size), and because many human beings now live reasonably safer lives, at least when it comes to predators, than we did tens of thousands of years ago, this negativity bias transfers itself onto other, less physically threatening scenarios. In media, bad news usually makes better clickbait than good, as minor irritations, complaints, and schadenfreude rise above good news in the hierarchy of your consciousness. The human nervous system often functions more like an overly sensitive burglar alarm than a reliable barometer of the weather. One telling example of negativity bias: let's say someone sends you an e-mail with personal feedback about your work, and their feedback includes nine major compliments and one minor critique. Your mind ignores the multiple compliments and focuses on the lone criticism. Why?

This bias toward negativity also affects how we perceive, in the present moment, our relationship to the members of our families. When Grandpa Sol was around, for example, I might have had exactly the same response that Fred Savage had to seeing his grandfather so often: disinterested and bratty complaints about having to read a book rather than getting to play his video game. Now, in retrospect, every single moment with each of my long-lost grandparents seems exceedingly precious, and more so each day. Free from the momentary reactiveness of my nervous system to their physical presence, no longer bombarded by the drizzle of minor irritants and awkward duties of interaction, the explicit memories of my grandparents have been slowly reprinted with brightness and affection. This realization that my ability to appreciate my family has often been lacking has made me feel uncomfortably similar to the Grandson character, which is why I bristled at my friend's comparison. I didn't like the fact that I was (at least) as unaware of my good fortune as the Grandson was. I didn't accept the fact that I, too, have been the worst roommate in the world. It is a difficult lesson, one that might bring shame with it—to realize that you are the inheritor of many privileges in this life, and that those privileges haven't necessarily helped you achieve happiness. Thankfully, my teachers have encouraged me to counteract this negativity, to learn to contemplate my own precious human life not as a tool of shame, but as a foundation of positivity, a base from which both personal awakening and care for others can proceed.

The Tibetan Buddhist system begins with a series of contemplations beautifully designed to rebalance the negativity bias. Within the classical Tibetan curriculum, before a person engaged in any further Tantric meditations, the first step was to spend time in recurring contemplation on gratitude for one's human life. This contemplation included thinking about the harmful circumstances from which the practitioner was free, and the helpful circumstances, or privileges, the practitioner possessed. Contemplating these freedoms and privileges was intended to provoke a confrontation, bringing the practitioner face-to-face with the prominence of complaint in the mind, while slowly building an acknowledgment of the precious opportunity of one's current situation, a positive urgency to use their time wisely. Urgency without anxiety is crucial to any transformation, and this inspiration would launch their dharma practice with vigor.

You can think of the set of practices collectively called contemplative meditation as a productive struggle, a gentle grappling with a particular fact of life. These practices of deep, directive thinking form the basis for later contemplation on lineage. In the first contemplative meditation on precious human life, you struggle to recognize that you have supportive circumstance for living an awakened life, such as having your sense perceptions and mental faculties intact and not being born in a place of imminent danger or war, with enough free time to consider the meaning of life and the freedom to set intentions for how you spend your limited time here. One such contemplation involves repeating the following phrases and considering their meaning within the quiet and space of meditation: "Joyful to have such a human life," "Difficult to find," "Free," and "Well-favored." "Difficult to find" reminds us of the unfathomable number and types of sentient beings who don't have the luxury of a human existence on this earth. "Free" refers to a contemplation of the difficult human experiences from which you are free. "Well-favored" signifies thinking in depth about the positive advantages and privileges your particular human life has offered. Traditional contemplative meditation involves a list of eighteen freedoms and advantages (for example, not being born in a war zone, having a healthy body, having a certain level of education) that a person might mull over to overcome complaint.

This contemplation of gratitude and privilege was never meant to invoke shame at your good fortune, or make you feel overwhelmed by whatever difficult circumstances you may inherit. Even I have often turned this contemplation into a way to beat myself up. For example, I've contemplated that I received an amazing education only to still be confused about how to act in the world's class dynamics. Frequently, I hear those of us who live in the Kale Belt creating a new kind of self-aggression out of our relative "well-favored" position in the world. For example, let's say your middle-class home in Portland suddenly floods. With gratitude in mind, trying to keep your suffering in perspective, you might say something about the difficulties of others, such as "Well, at least I am not in Syria right now."

This is an attempt to put your own suffering in context, which is always a good thing, especially when your nervous system causes you to feel endangered by something that's not life-threatening. However, "At least I am not in Syria right now" is not actually a contemplation of gratitude. For one thing, it alone doesn't lead you to do much that is helpful for the plight of Syrians, and it also doesn't necessarily lead you toward appreciation for your opportunity to be mindful and compassionate right here and now, in the midst of the flood. The contemplation of precious human life was not meant to generate further shame at resolvable complaints and momentary irritations. Rather, it was meant to invoke a quiet gratitude, and even joy, alongside a sense of opportunity. Then maybe we could do something small yet concrete to help Syria.

In working with family, touching upon basic optimism about where you come from is more accurate than you might believe. The energy necessary to pursue awakening requires a lot of accurate positive intention and view. If positive thinking is vague and generic, it becomes nothing more than useless platitudes, like telling someone to "cheer up" while their house is flooding. But positivity becomes accuracy when we realize we are abnormally tilted toward negativity due to our biological inheritance. When we see that we are geared toward misperceiving threats, focusing on difficulties because of the exaggerations of the nervous system, something powerful can shift. Out of the gratitude of contemplation, you start to complain less about things that don't really matter, which saves a surprising amount of energy. And if you want to deal with difficult family relationships, you will need that energy.

Gratitude can be as simple as gently forcing yourself to dwell a bit longer, even a few extra seconds, on the positive experiences that come from ordinary sense perceptions, which are also a part of your family inheritance.

Chögyam Trungpa often talked about experiencing

basic goodness in a very childlike way. He would say things like "We can appreciate vividness: the yellowness of yellow, the redness of red, the greenness of green, the purpleness of purple."[1] Depending on how you look at it, this quote is either incredibly profound dharma or a series of wasted and redundant words. I can imagine myself, as the Grandson, rolling my eyes at the total lameness of this instruction. (*Really, Grandpa? The purpleness of purple?*) I can see my own face scrunched at how "dumb" these words might sound. I see my younger self not appreciating the irony at all, fidgeting away from the vivid colors naturally surrounding me on all sides, returning with a meditative absorption to the preprogrammed purples and reds and greens of my Nintendo game. To take, say, ten seconds to appreciate the colors in the boring room that surrounds you as you read, to allow extra time for the spectrum of light currently entering your retina to affect you as imaginatively as it wants to, to acknowledge that the five senses themselves are a familial inheritance transmitted with great love from parent to child, is a contemplation of your precious human life. And these ten seconds of visual gratitude will literally make you feel better.

This sense of humble gratitude becomes crucial whenever you turn your attention to the events of your family history. Often, it may feel like history is aligned against you. Even if your grandparents and parents passed along to you neuroses, abandonment, and trauma, at the very least they brought you into a world where you have your sense perceptions, your motor skills, the ability to think, the ability to feel your emotions. Even if some of these skills feel impaired or blocked, even if some of them cause you to act destructively, much of what we inherit is an inexhaustible treasure chest. To begin to appreciate the stories of your family, *The Princess Brides* of your own lineage, is to start to open that vault. We must retrain to see the positive impact that our lineage has had upon us, especially if we want to pass along a mindful and beneficial environment to our own children and grandchildren.

Having engaged in this formal meditation contemplation for many years, I must say it has helped me get over some things, or at least make significant progress in working through them. I get caught less often in the complaints that arise from privilege and self-absorption. Many of us live with a kind of "latte suffering,"[2] an inner environment of complaint about each minor inconvenience which perpetuates an unwillingness to accept reality as it is. The practice of gratitude has helped me not worry so much if life's tiny comforts are not on my side today. Gratitude, as a practice, makes for a lower-maintenance human being.

Deepening the notion of precious human life, the Shambhala teachings use chants, ceremony, visualization, contemplation, and social interactions to form a relationship with lineage, both your own family lineages and your larger cultural lineages of authentic leadership. It is by cradling your practice of awakening within an ongoing connection to lineage that you begin to feel at home with your human inheritance.

Your Three Lineages:
Inheriting Karma, Inheriting Wisdom

IN ALL OF BUDDHISM'S RELATIONAL meditation practices, the benefactor connects you to one of your lineages. In the Shambhala tradition, three overarching aspects of lineage are emphasized: the mother lineage, the father lineage, and the ancestral lineage. This triad is made up of complementary aspects of your wisdom inheritance. Practitioners use these three lineages in study and practice to invoke a sense of connection, support, and personal empowerment for the journey. There is both a literal and a more energetic description of each of these three aspects of lineage.

First, as the classic Tibetan contemplation on benefactors reminds us, is your mother lineage. Taken literally, the mother lineage represents the wisdom we each inherit from our mothers, and from the maternal side of our families. Honoring the mother lineage would include paying tribute to the culture, ethnicity, religion, and wisdom of your mother's family and ancestors as representations of your human inheritance. This would involve studying them and symbolically incorporating them into your spiritual practice in some way.

Addressing the topic more metaphorically, the mother lineage represents the energy of the mind that is related to space and insight, the nurturing openness to accommodate whatever thought arises within your awareness, the gentle environment needed for wisdom to arise and for clarity to grow. Awareness and gentleness are the internal mother lineage. In symbolism, the mother lineage represents those beings or cultural icons who have given you examples of this sort of gentleness and accommodating wisdom, those who have learned how to hold the space for clarity to arise.

Similarly, the father lineage includes all the spiritual and cultural inheritances of your father's family that you incorporate into your practice. Moreover, the father lineage refers to all the benefactors representing fearless action and skillful means when it is time to do something brave in the world. In daily life, the father lineage is about daring and taking chances. Every break from the status quo of habit requires some bravery, and in the Tibetan system, the masculine form of energy is equated with knowing how to engage at exactly the right moment to get a job done.

When we discuss these masculine and feminine lineages, we are not looking at identified genders of people or physical embodiments, but rather at qualities of energy. Just as a battery has a masculine component and a feminine component, which together generate its full power, and just as many wisdom systems have looked at the balance of complementary energies (such as yin and yang, or rajas, tamas, and sattva), the masculine and feminine energies of lineage are complementary aspects of your emotional makeup. The mother and father lineages swim together in your being, collaborating to create an integrated person. In Tantra, someone who identifies as male might have tremendous feminine energy, just as someone who identifies as female can be part of the father lineage, depending on the kind of wisdom they embody and pass along. Ultimately, the lineages mix together to create intelligent confidence—confidence you can access whenever you remember the inheritance of your lineage.

The third lineage represents the wisdom of societal and cultural inheritance for whatever you are pursuing as your life's work. Your ancestors, or ancestral lineage,[3] refers to all the heroes and benefactors of your interests in the world, especially those ancestors who were skilled leaders, helping to bring about a more compassionate culture in their own time and place. In the Shambhala lineage, these include any previous leaders of society who brought wisdom and compassion into being. A very early example of enlightened leadership discussed in Shambhala was the great Indian king Ashoka, who began as a violent tyrant but later, taken by the teachings of Buddhism, transformed his terrain into a compassionate land. The makeup of your ancestral lineage depends on the sort of work you do in the world. If, like me, you are a writer, then your lineage would include the writers you respect and admire from the past. If you work for social justice, then the great activists of the past could be contemplated. And if you are a musician, you might visualize recently passed ancestors named David Bowie and Prince.

Your Lineage Has Your Back

ALONG WITH ALL OUR NEGATIVITY toward the perceived threats of the present moment, we often move through the world feeling like the past has screwed us over. Yes, we have each inherited habitual patterns through the interwoven conduits of genes, parents, education, and culture. We have also inherited traumas based on past conflict and oppression. Today, a rising field of scientific inquiry called epigenetics explores how our environment, relationships, and inherited trauma affect the very expression of our genetic coding. Meditation is already being studied in relation to its influence on one's genes. It is not hard to imagine the study of one's heartfelt experience of spiritual lineage, or the absence of a connection with lineage, eventually being included in the gene study.

The Mama-*sattva*

RECALLING THE SUPPORT OF YOUR lineage by invoking benefactors is designed to change the framework for how you look at all you have inherited. Sometimes, as you work to generate compassion for both self and other in relational meditation practices, it's hard to think of a personal benefactor you really trust. It might be difficult to use direct human examples as your trusted benefactor, *especially* people from your family. "Don't meet your heroes," a famous expression goes.

Once you relate to humans in proximity, once you are close enough to "smell" them, they often display imperfections that trigger your mistrust too easily. The more intimately you know somebody, the more familiar (and familial) you become with their human flaws, the harder it becomes to see that person as a source of unconditional love. Sometimes even historical heroes you've never met seem inaccessible as embodiments of basic goodness. Revisionist histories tend to unveil the flaws of history's giants. Sometimes, in order to believe in basic goodness, you need a fantasy hero, a superhero, an archetype of love and wisdom.

To aid the process of unconditional trust, Tantric Buddhism uses figures who occupy a different frame of narrative existence from the humans we've known personally. These more archetypal benefactors are designed to counteract our fault-finding tendencies, to create a pillar of support in our consciousnesses. This sort of psychological archetype, a fairy-tale embodiment of wisdom, compassion, skillfulness, and other positive qualities, was the original meaning of the term *bodhisattva*.[4] These bodhisattvas are often imagined in energetic form, not as solid entities but as holograms of radiant light, positive projections generated by the mind. These bodhisattvas are not saviors but expressions of our highest qualities, and our recollection of them, or the reciting of a mantra associated with them, serves as support for the qualities we try to develop. Depending on the particular type of wisdom you are cultivating, the light and embodiment take on different shapes, colors, genders, and forms.

I am convinced that the bodhisattva's significance in Tantric cultures arose for the same reason that the comic-book and fairy-tale narratives of Western civilization did: to inspire us to find real courage via symbolism. We need to visualize bodhisattvas, just as we need to see heroes on the screen or page. Often, real people are too easily perceived as flawed to inspire us, especially the real people in our families. As one of my mentors and colleagues, Dr. Miles Neale, has said, these bodhisattvas create an awakened filter, a helpful set of "training wheels," which allow space for you not to get caught up in the perceived, or very real, shortcomings of your human mentors. You focus on bodhisattvas to help run the perceived imperfections of your real elders and mentors through a mental sieve, to gain confidence that your human leaders are, at their core, also pretty great. When you give someone genuine permission to be awesome, they might start to rise to the occasion, and then you begin to rise to the occasion in return.

About five years ago, a very unexpected thing happened with my imagined benefactor during one of these practices. On this particular morning, as I sat down to practice a version of loving-kindness meditation unfolding in stages, something new appeared. I invoked my lineage by reciting a chant to honor them, then closed my eyes and focused my attention on calling to mind a benefactor, a hero of loving-kindness. Guess who showed up, spontaneously and flawlessly vivid, like a 3D movie: my mother. This was a big surprise. Don't get me wrong; my mother often appears in my loving-kindness meditations. Usually she appears at the stage of practice in which I work to generate greater empathy toward a loved one. Occasionally, when times have been hard between us, Mom appeared in the stage of practice done for an irritating or emotionally difficult person. I'm sure I've appeared similarly in her practice throughout the years.

But that day, she showed up in a totally different form, in a new light. Here was a grand female figure sitting cross-legged in the space in front of my mind's eye on a pristine lotus flower. The figure was smiling with strength and power, radiating silky waves of moonlight from her heart center, as if she were an unwavering source of lunar power, power that was both soothing and invigorating to my heart. There was no flaw in my perception of this being, merely a new way of beholding her. She had many of the same symbolic qualities as the classic bodhisattva Tara, such as youthful elegance mixing with a wisdom behind her eyes that seemed to push back to the dawn of time. But this was not Tara: this being had my mother's face and presence. This was the Mama-*sattva*.

In my younger years, as any son might, I viewed my mother as a complicated entity, a source of both attraction and aversion to the spiritual path I was on. Sometimes, like now, our relationship has been extremely close, and sometimes it has hit roadblocks. We even took breaks from speaking to each other. As with any two family members, we have occasionally reminded each other, unintentionally, of those things we'd rather forget. I reminded her of a man who hurt her, and she reminded me of a home in which I held no power.

But on this particular morning, Mom reminded me only of the depth of my human potential. She appeared in a form of total wisdom and strength, manifesting her deepest underlying nature. Suddenly, from this powerful image of her awakened essence, I plugged into a newfound respect for my mother's bravery, and its place in my three lineages.

Hopefully, we all have those stories of the courageous triumphs of our lineage. I already had images of the bravery of my spiritual "ancestors," especially the young Trungpa Rinpoche's harrowing and traumatic escape from the developing genocide in the Kham region of eastern Tibet. After his miraculous arrival in the West, he was still adamant in proclaiming that "basic goodness" was the nature of humanity. I had stories of the bravery of my father lineage: hearing how Grandpa Sol, as a (too) young military doctor in World War II helped with the primary liberation of the Dachau concentration camp, and then treated many sick and wounded there. And now the Mama-*sattva* had helped me recall the power of my mother lineage, even if no genocide was involved in the quieter braveries of Mom's personal saga. I saw her courage in moving from a small southern town to the bankrupt badlands of New York City in the early 1970s, knowing no one, in order to start a career in visual arts. I witnessed her later bravery at figuring out how to make life work as a single mother in an unforgiving city. I recalled her decision to switch careers in her fifties and take a big leap to start her professional life all over again, returning to school, becoming a psychotherapist, and choosing to help many more people work with their minds.

When the Mama-*sattva* appeared in my practice as a strong, capable, and pristine benefactor of loving-kindness, it said more about something shifting within my own heart than anything about her. At the time, I was in Texas, and Mom was two thousand miles away from me, in Massachusetts. She had no idea she was appearing in my awareness. For that moment, I was able to recover my faith in her human strength and wisdom, her Buddha nature, which already existed. Her body was literally my first home on this earth, and she protected me when I was utterly defenseless. Without her patient (and forgotten) instructions, even a spoon would have been too complicated an instrument for my neural network to comprehend. Given all these truths, connecting deeply with Mom's awakened nature was a crucial step for feeling my own goodness, my secure attachment to planet Earth. With this image of her as a bodhisattva warrior, I had an experience of her that was awake, healed, and totally workable.

The mother, father, and ancestral lineages were now all present and offering their support to my consciousness, even if their bodies were absent. I am telling this story not because I expect the same to happen to you. It's possible that your own relationship with your mother, or another figure from your mother, father, or ancestral lineages, is more difficult to relate to than the one I've described. Or it's possible that your mother has always been your clearest benefactor. It might take a while before you can practice loving-kindness toward your mother, or it might be effortless.

Either way, the blockages in your connection with each of your three lineages can be slowly healed in your own heart, and you can come to build trust in your family's inherited goodness, wisdom, and strength. All sentient beings have been your mother, all have been Grandpa. All have taken a turn as your protector. The wisdom of your social and cultural ancestors, both recent and historic, is available in the present moment. In fact, if you permit a long enough scope of time, every relationship can become more pliant, softened, and workable. Even if some of the work happens in the next "lifetime," that's okay.

When I was in fourth grade, both my family and spiritual lineages experienced moments of sudden collapse. Everyone inherits obstacles, but if you focus only on the confusion and trauma of your inheritance, you end up moving through the world with a defeatist attitude, preprogrammed toward negativity. So often, we wake up in the morning feeling that the past is lined up against us, that the function of history is to screw us over in the present. What's the point of even getting out of bed, then? As we struggle through each day from this perspective, we feel imprisoned by our inheritance. Contemplating and connecting with the mother, father, and ancestral lineages allows a shift. It's not about a perfect relationship with those who came before, because those who came before had issues, of course. Rather, it's about feeling like you don't need to fight your past. It often feels as if we're each in a duel against our personal histories. But when you form a connection with your wisdom lineage, suddenly, amazingly, the past has your back. Despite whatever grief I still carry, I know my imperfect lineage has my back. And this means that I can begin to have the future's back. On that basis, I can show up and work with family, just like everything else, as a practice. I can now become someone else's benefactor. Eventually, perhaps, I will become Grandpa myself. And that is how a lineage continues.

As You Wish, Part II

The Practice of Family

MANY OF THE RELATIONAL PRACTICES AND TEACH-
ings that might apply to friendship and romance will also
apply to family. If you buy the assumption that family is
the hardest space in relational practice, then you might
need some extra tips to create mindfulness and compassion in the time spent with your family. Again, the special
problem with family is the entangling of karmic patterns:

how uncomfortably similar the "other" is to you, in history, genes, and habits. Your habitual tendencies get knotted up with those of your family like a ball of rubber bands. It's hard to maintain perspective and clarity about what is actually happening in your own mind versus what is happening for someone else. If you don't know what is happening in your own mind (if you can't feel it, note it, and acknowledge it), then mindfulness has little basis to begin. Time spent with family is like throwing a party where everyone gets drunk (and then hung over) off each other's fermented karma. The whole thing can be messy, irritating, and claustrophobic. There's only one way to practice mindfulness when you're intoxicated by karma: slow down the pace of every interaction so that mindfulness can develop.

Listening: Finding Someone's *Princess Bride* Moment

I HAVE YET TO MEET a human being who does not appreciate being heard. With family members, this sometimes means listening to people with whom you feel you have little in common. This lack of commonality is one of the most painful aspects of family: to feel so distant in makeup and interests from those with whom you share the most biological information. Differences with those whom look like you might create intense feelings of aloneness; it's why such an abnormal proportion of humans throughout history have wondered if they were adopted. But commonality and difference in interests can and should coexist, just as they do in friendship and romance. In family dynamics, listening is often the greatest act of diplomacy, the best tool at your disposal. Sometimes listening is the only thing you can do, especially when there is not much (perceived) common ground. Without some shared language of experience, nothing else is possible, especially not the expression of disappointment or hurt feelings. If you don't even know what a person enjoys, they probably aren't going to be open to hearing the ways they've hurt you. If you know you aren't willing to listen, it's going to be impossible to relate.

"Everybody loves something, even if it is only tortillas." This quote by Chögyam Trungpa is a reminder that relational trust is built upon listening. I have discovered a new articulation of that teaching: *Everybody loves something, even if it is only* The Princess Bride. Listening allows for the discovery of another person's *Princess Bride* moment. Not only does listening increase intelligence, but it also creates a basis for shared experience. If you cannot find common ground with someone, if you don't even know what they are interested in, then a real relationship can't ever develop. Without trust, giving someone feedback on the things that aren't working, saying the things you really need to say, is rendered more challenging, if possible at all. The discovery of another person's *Princess Bride* moment is an act of commitment to family.

You win a lot of allies simply by inquiring about someone's genuine interests and formative cultural moments while actively holding the person in your attention. For example, it might be better to sit down on the couch next to your cousin and ask him to explain to you the rules of

NASCAR, rather than dive straight into a divisive conversation about politics. This practice probably won't make you a NASCAR fan—I've already tried—but it will at least create the foundation for some mutual respect. Your cousin will at least feel he is a real person in your eyes. Many parents throughout history are the most selfless examples of this sort of immersion in someone else's interests. Out of this weird thing called unconditional love, parents adopt the interests of their children, investing themselves in hobbies, art forms, sports, and other activities they never thought they would be caught near. How many so-called soccer moms were into soccer before they became moms? Various biological and spiritual signals tell them, "This is my child. I have to love this person no matter what, so let's see what they are all about."

Recently, after discussing with Mandy Patinkin this project and his *Time* magazine piece, I gave myself this thought experiment: What would I do if my own cousin were someone whose worldview was as hard to digest as that of Sen. Ted Cruz? Ted Cruz, in fact, is a cousin of mine, a relative residing well beyond the degrees of removal that normally categorize the branches of family trees. Have you ever wondered how many degrees of familial separation you must be from another person for them to be excluded from your definition of family? Is a fourth cousin still your family? A tenth cousin? How many billions of cousins are there on earth? How many biological degrees am I separated from my very furthest human relative?

I know that Cousin Ted and I disagree on a lot: health care, women's rights, economic issues, Black Lives Matter, gun control, and the catastrophe of climate change. If my practice were strong when I met Cousin Ted, I probably would not begin our conversation by sharing my heartfelt belief that he is wrong about pretty much everything. The attempt to "school" him wouldn't be helpful for either of us—he might school me, in fact—and it might end any hope of our understanding each other. Instead, I might ask Cousin Ted to tell me about the first time he saw *The Princess Bride*. "How old were you? Who were you with? What kind of candy did you eat? Exactly how stuck in your teeth did the Jujubes get? Popcorn—with or without butter? Do you remember what you thought about the Grandfather? Did he remind you of your own grandpa, too? Which grandpa? And will you do your Miracle Max impression for me?"

Listening to family members with whom you don't have much in common also leads to the flip side of listening: expressing yourself. There comes a time to speak your own interests to your family, your own way of being in the world, your own social and political values. Students sometimes ask me how they might go about explaining their meditation practice to family members. Some people feel a sense of isolation because they are the only ones in their families interested in meditation or Buddhism. They're afraid their families think they're weirdos. Out of this fear, they often assume that their families don't want to hear anything about it. This hesitation to share can be a self-fulfilling prophecy, though: if you aren't willing to share with your family what is important to you, it may create further isolation and separation, and a further feeling, from them, that you're the one who is not interested in connecting with them.

Just as you might be open to listening to your family members' *Princess Bride* moments, you could also be confidently unapologetic about sharing your own interests. Sharing the practices that mean something to you is not about preaching or proselytizing, not about convincing anyone else that they need to be doing what you're doing. Instead, it allows those close to you to see what your life is like, what moves you. If you feel that you have already tried to share your practice and gotten nowhere, then perhaps the practice you need is to take more space apart, contemplating precious human life and appreciation for your lineage, so that the frustration and sadness of isolation from those closest to you can be placed in a context of general gratitude for your humanity.

Taking Space

HOW DOES A PERSON KNOW HOW *much* of any practice they can handle? The key to longevity with any practice is knowing when to lean in and when to step back. For example, sometimes I am just too emotionally burdened to meditate for the full amount of time my daily practice guidelines dictate. So, instead, I choose to practice for five to ten minutes, or take a mindful walk around the block. One of my friends, a meditation teacher and filmmaker named John Ankele, says that on the days you are emotionally or logistically unable to practice, you should still take the time to bow to your meditation cushion, if only to remember that it's there. Bowing to your meditation seat is a way to honor what the ritual of practice means for you, even when you can't practice.

Many people report, with both hesitation and shame, that they have a hard time dealing with certain family members for more than a very short period of time. Their family lives involve a complex set of evasive maneuvers, avoiding phone calls and excusing themselves from invitations to prolonged visits. There's nothing wrong with taking a little space and knowing how much practice with family you can reasonably handle. When you allow yourself to set the working parameters of your own relationships, you are practicing self-compassion. When you decide that you need to focus on relating to yourself, you are practicing self-care.

When it comes to family, the biggest obstacle facing meditators is the unrealistic expectation that our practice is supposed to make us invincible. We often feel like we should be able to handle anything and everything. Because we have some relationship with our own minds, sometimes we think that we *should* be superheroes when it comes to dealing with difficult circumstances. We *should* dive in to family, and no difficulty *should* be able overcome us. But *shoulds* have nothing to do with being mindful. We each need to be skillful, reasonable, and compassionate toward our own limitations. Fearlessness is about working at the edge of our limitations; recklessness is about ignoring those boundaries. Sometimes difficult family relationships and what they provoke in you deliver you past the edge of reasonable practice.

Just as we do when the practice of meditation gets too difficult, we might take a bit of space and approach the practice of family from a new direction. If a family member with whom you have a hard time asks you to come for a four-day visit—an intensive four-day retreat with your own claustrophobic karma: yay!—you might decide to visit them for the afternoon instead. Knowing how much practice you can handle is the key to self-compassion. It's okay to make things easy on yourself, and if you are honest about what you can handle, shortened periods of time spent with family can feel like growth instead of regression.

Sometimes, taking space means making a conscious decision not to interact with a member of your family at all for the time being. While this might seem like a letdown, a failure to engage boldly with difficult circumstances, it might also be a thoughtful choice, a recognition that the relationship causes you harm. If you decide to take more long-term space from a member of your family, I would advise keeping them in your meditation practice whenever you can, occasionally bringing them to mind and generating loving-kindness, or struggling with practicing forgiveness for them, making the clear aspiration that when the time is right, even if that time is years or lifetimes away, you hope to reestablish a relationship with that person.

Forgiveness

JUST AS GENEROSITY IS AN act of letting go via offering, the practice of forgiveness is a way to release the stuckness of resentment's hold over your mind. Resentment is the most subtle and corrosive form of hatred. It blocks your emotional arteries. Generosity and forgiveness are both about relinquishing the vise grip on whatever you are holding on to, which means that both are acts of purification. Generosity is a helpful practice with chosen friends with whom you already have a mutually trusting relationship, or with those strangers with whom you have less at stake. If the family member is also a trusted friend, then you might be able to offer to them freely, to establish a mutual process of letting go of your own agenda in order to accommodate their needs. You might be able to bring them flowers, or just give them your time. Like a healthy friendship, a healthy family relationship includes letting go and engaging in mutual sacrifice.

Forgiveness is a personal practice of letting go, an internal effort to heal resentments when hurt and pain are still being carried. If the practice of generosity isn't possible, you can always prepare your mental landscape by engaging in a meditation on forgiveness.

Within the body of Buddhist meditations geared toward relationships, a three-step meditation on forgiveness taught by Jack Kornfield and others has been one of the most helpful practices for me, especially within the realm of family. In this three-step process, you first sit with your breath for a few minutes. Then you bring to mind an instance when you harmed someone. It could be a very simple act you regret, such as stepping in front of someone in a grocery checkout line or saying something sarcastic during a work meeting. If you feel ready, you could work with actions of yours that caused more harm. (Given that it is thirty years later, I have been able to bring my fourth-grade friend to mind in this practice, and request his forgiveness for rejecting him.) You practice holding in mind the mistake you made, the harm you caused, and simply request forgiveness, paying attention to the sensations in your body as you ponder the harm and make the request. The ability to request forgiveness is based entirely on belief in basic goodness, belief that mistakes are not condemnations, but rather teachable moments. Even to request forgiveness is an act of maturity, because the request is an acknowledgment that mistakes are inevitable to human life.

Second, you bring to mind a way you have harmed yourself. You practice offering yourself forgiveness, again paying attention to the sensations in your body when you generate the wish.

Finally, you bring to mind the actions of someone who harmed you, and you practice offering that person forgiveness, letting go of the residue of confusion and resentment that their actions caused you. Again, you stay present with whatever sensations or feelings arise in the process. This practice can be repeated as needed in regular meditation. It may take weeks, months, or years to feel much noticeable release of resentment or shame.

It is often hard to forgive because our minds make a very classic blunder, gluing together two entities that are, in reality, distinct—compassion and agreement. We often think that if we are compassionate toward someone, we are admitting that that they are completely right, which in turn further empowers their harmful behavior. But compassion is not an empowerment of a person's actions; it is only an admission that the person is also human. Offering someone forgiveness does not mean you are empowering his version of reality. You can offer a family member or an ex-partner forgiveness while making the tough choice not to speak to them for the foreseeable future. You can offer the CEO of a corporation compassion while you lead a boycott of their company. You can wish for your cousin Ted Cruz to discover boundless heaps of personal joy and fulfillment, and then go register thousands of people to vote for his opponent.

Unconditional Love

UNLIKE MARRIAGE, THERE IS NO vow for family. Perhaps your birth, a passport-free arrival on earth, was your implicit vow to your family. Whatever vow might be required for you to exist in a family, you have already taken it. It is highly unclear whether we choose our families. Classic Tibetan thought is surprisingly Oedipal on this point. It claims that your disembodied consciousness is energetically attracted to your birth parents as they make love.[1] When it comes to why any of us arrived here, *choose* is a very delicate word, based on a premise with many variables hidden behind it. *Choice* points to the complexities of free will, the volitions we control, and the many interwoven circumstances we do not. It doesn't really matter whether you chose your birth. What matters is that you use the uniqueness of this human inheritance, and cultivate appreciation for your specific family lineages as the training ground for awakening in this life. To embrace your family as an aspect of practice is to embrace your accountability to lineage, which is the key to your own awakening. "As you wish," that mantra of true love and devotion, is about a loyalty to family that transcends the ups and downs of individual interactions.

Even though family may be the hardest practice, that doesn't mean it isn't a worthwhile practice. As long as you remember that taking space is always a valid act, the contemplation of your lineage and closest relationships will always be fruitful. This contemplation can also give you the confidence to find your own voice, prominent and particular, within your lineage.

Conclusion

Have Fun Storming the Castle

THE MOST IMPORTANT EPISODE IN THE MULTIFAC-
eted biography of Siddhartha Gautama is told far too rarely.
It's a story of the future Buddha as an adult, just a few
months and a few narrative footsteps away from his complete awakening. The story is a simple flash, just a moment
in time. The episode points directly to a kind of nostalgia
we've all experienced, that moment an adult remembers

what it is like to be a child. The ancient texts tell of Siddhartha's rediscovery of his own basic goodness, although the original discourse does not use such language. At age thirty-five, this man is close to the end of his quest. His determination to confront reality has been admirable, to say the least. For the past six years, he's been in relentless pursuit of a stable understanding of his own mind and a panoramic awareness of the world of sentient beings. During this time, he has been striving with intense discipline and massive sacrifices, remaining outside the confines of his former life in society. He has studied deeply with several masters a transcendental style of meditation, and has engaged in grueling feats of self-denial. He has tools both for yogic discipline and for a most powerful concentration. But the states of mind he has mastered seem either too constructed, and therefore prone to impermanence, or else too harsh and punitive, fueling more of the same self-aggression that he set out to overcome. And now, just as he gives up on the extreme practice of self-denial that taught him great discipline but led to unnecessary punishment, he has a simple memory.

As if visualizing, the thirty-five-year-old nomad is instantly a child again, age nine. As if then were now, as if now were *always*, the man viscerally inhabits the child's awareness, open and receptive. The nine-year-old boy is sitting under a rose apple tree, next to the fields at his father's estate. He is watching the workers plow the soil. In this spot, the boy feels safe and comfortable, fully alive. He feels at home. He touches a relaxed presence, a knowing that expands inward and outward at the same time. It is as if the nine-year-old boy within were already meditating, without any effort, perceiving the current moment with curiosity and innocence. When the recollection fades, the man Siddhartha moves on, but he keeps the memory with him. The memory becomes an anchor of the final leg of his awakening as a Buddha. What the thirty-five-year-old remembers is that true presence is not some chore or task. Rather, awareness is an inheritance of one's birth into the human family. Awakening is an expression of natural innocence, the innocence that already *was-is-will-be*.

This childhood memory sparks a powerful recognition of the unconditional aspect of mind, an awareness that accommodates every moment, even when the person doesn't have a clue what to *do* with the moment yet. In the coming months, the grown-up Siddhartha uses this childhood memory, combined with the disciplines and meditative skills he has already learned. His insights begin to move forward by leaps and bounds. The recollection of this childhood innocence, alongside the rigor and discipline he has already achieved, create the circumstances for his final awakening.

Even though he was sitting under a rose apple tree, let's not make the mistake of lifting rose-colored glasses to our eyes. Siddhartha wasn't exactly recalling a "happier" time back in the day. The life he led as a nine-year-old was far from idyllic, even if it was blessed by wealth. His mother died in childbirth, and his father, by most accounts, was a controlling narcissist. Human life was hard, far harder than for a privileged person now, and life expectancy in the Iron Age was much shorter than it is now, even when compared to that in the very poorest countries of the modern-day world.[1] Suffering and trauma were all around this nine-year-old boy.

This memory of ease and connection that revisits the thirty-five-year-old Siddhartha is not some perfect moment of bliss, no easy whitewashing of a yesteryear. Rather, as Siddhartha recovers from his very grown-up bout of self-aggression, pushing himself too hard against his own humanity, he recalls his inherent innocence. In the midst of confusion, chaos, and trauma, he reclaims a moment of presence, a moment of human goodness that he neither created nor had to earn. His innocence is not indebted to anyone or anything. It doesn't appear only when life is great. Innocence does not stand in opposition to life's chaos. Instead, Siddhartha recalls the innocence that abides *within* chaos.

This journey leads us to something that does not need to be created, something we already possess. We already *are* aware. We already *were* worthy. And we always *will be* innocent.

Nine is an interesting age in relation to the perception of innocence, isn't it? It's a very awkward moment in the process of our emergence as social creatures. When you're nine or ten, people aren't thinking of you as a cute little kid anymore; nor are they treating you like an empowered adult yet, either. In relation to self-identity, nine is a limbo period, a *bardo*, a space sandwiched between the forgiving cuteness of early childhood and the harsh "you-break-it-you-buy-it" accountabilities yet to come. For me, nine was the most chaotic and destabilizing limbo of childhood. Yet, when I contemplate a moment similar to Siddhartha's under that rose apple tree, I am always drawn back to a connected moment within that chaos, that June day sitting on a bench in Riverside Park with my grandfather and parents. In that moment, all four of us were deeply dissatisfied with our current life circumstances, yet still content to be a family, together for just one more moment under the forgiving shade of an elm tree.

This path offers no escape from chaos or pain. If you don't develop sympathy for your own chaos, you won't be able to help anyone else. Soon after remembering my own moment under the elm tree, I think of my connection to *The Princess Bride* again. *The Princess Bride* is not really a comedy, although it starts out that way. On every level, the movie is a wacky transmission of true love. True love is not an idea; it is the feeling of having a shared story. Perhaps that is why, as I grow older, I become even more nostalgic with regard to this film, and why its popularity continues to grow in the world. The movie reconnects me fully to basic goodness. I do not believe I am alone in this feeling.

At its very best, lineage is the transmission of those stories that remind you of your own bravery. My tradition, Shambhala, transmits its own fairy tale, about a mythical kingdom of the same name, a kingdom that supposedly existed at the time of the Buddha. The king and queen of this place, known later as the Rigdens of Shambhala, were no Trumperdincks. These leaders were openhearted, wise, and skillful. They invited the Buddha, later in his life, when he dedicated himself only to the teaching of others, to visit them. They asked the Buddha to give teachings for those of us who did not want to become monastic or leave the world behind for a cave. The Buddha supposedly gave the king, queen, and their court special teachings on the nature of mind and the nature of a harmonious society, teachings he had not given his monks. He taught a path of awakening within the turmoil of society, provided instructions on how to use societal relations as the vehicle for enlightenment. Shambhala, the myth says, soon became an enlightened kingdom. Its politics, art, culture, and economics were all executed with mindfulness and compassion. Goodness, interdependence, and sustainability were the underlying principles of the land.

I started teaching Buddhism in 2002 because my practice had helped me begin to navigate the confusion and awkwardness of being myself. I did not start teaching because I had any personal interest in religion, and I was especially averse to both blind faith and spiritual mythologies. For this reason, when I was newer to teaching meditation, I would often hesitate to tell the story of Shambhala as a place, because the origin story of my tradition, a mythology that Chögyam Trungpa carried in his heart during his nearly impossible escape from Tibet, was nothing but a Himalayan fairy tale. None of Shambhala's historical existence could be verified, and I didn't really see the point of sharing it. Most of the people I was working with as a student, colleague, and teacher weren't really into myths, either, I gleaned. We were into studying the mind, not religion. We were into experience, not faith. We were into contemporary culture, not history. We were of the twenty-first century, not the ancient world.

What was the point of retelling the very *un*ironic, very *pre*modern fairy tale of Shambhala? That story didn't even have any funny parts, no lines to be quoted and converted into awesome memes. The story didn't even have any *kissing* parts. Why would anyone care about my family's inherited mythologies?

Eventually I realized why the fairy tale really did matter. First, the Shambhala fairy tale, about a community of people pursuing spiritual awakening *within* society, as a society, was a useful mythology indeed. Told properly, the story could inspire us that Shambhala was, in fact, this place right here. If we used these teachings to awaken in the world, Shambhala could even be this American spot. That flipping of the script, allowing fantasies to illuminate your reality rather than using them to escape it, is worthy of martial arts masters. This is a trick that so many storytellers throughout history has strived to achieve. People consume stories in order to escape their lives, but what if their reasoning changes? What if people consume stories in order to illuminate their lives? If fantasy illuminates reality, then escapes become road maps back to direct experience. And then all paths lead to awakening.

This same flip from family mythology into a life lesson is what the Grandfather achieves for his Grandson when he utters the movie's last line, "As you wish." True love is not about Florin versus Guilder. And really, kiddo, trust me, there is no Buttercup. True love is right here in Evanston, Illinois. True love was right there in Riverside Park.

That was the same voyage, from mythology back to reality, that my lineage was inviting me to take as it presented me with its own crazy fairy tale about a Himalayan kingdom. Shambhala was not some mountainous myth; it was a vision of a society where people knew how to treat each other, via personal, interpersonal, and collective systems of mindfulness. That society could be this society. Enlightened society is right here, if we want it to be.

As. We. Wish.

Maybe I'm just getting older myself. By the time you read this, I will be contemplating the stories I want to tell to my own child. My own crop of hair has embarked on a slow harvest of gray. It is unclear if I trade in each dark follicle for any silvery insight, but I hope so. As I further my investment in family and lineage, as I deepen my vows, I also further my investment in the stories of my spiritual tradition, even if I have always been fiercely secular and scientific about my Buddhist practice. I have grown proud to tell the tale of my lineage, complete with its Himalayan palaces and crystal castles that never existed, yet still wait to be stormed.

Before sitting down to meditate, it might help to take a moment to reflect on the stories inherited from your own lineage, especially the stories that came to you when you were a child. These mythologies are the fertile soil from which will ripen the stories of whatever you long to create, those stories to be updated, reinterpreted, deconstructed, and, above all else, shared.

I don't think we'll ever wake up without honoring the spiritual value of modern culture, because the act of awakening will always occur within the context of one's own culture. Modern culture is only a click or a tap away, and it's too stamped on our psyches (like a tattoo we don't remember why we got) for us ever to abandon now. If there are even any caves left in which to hide away from the world, those caves are currently being wired for the Internet. Pop culture has become a spiritual text in and of itself, and I fully embrace that fact.

Of course I want to discuss the dharma of ancient meditation, metaphysics, ethics, and psychology, for sure. If you are interested, I cover these topics in *The Road Home: A Contemporary Exploration of the Buddhist Path.* But I also want to discuss the dharma of stand-up comedy, the dharma of abstract expressionism, the dharma of Wes Anderson movies, the dharma of magical realism, and the dharma of Missy Elliott. And I especially want to discuss why mindful people belong on the front lines of any movement counteracting racism, sexism, poverty, and the catastrophe of climate change. Because all these things exist, they all must exist in our practice. Contemporary culture must become fully integrated into our spiritual lives, unless we want both culture and spirituality to become only parallel ceremonies of escapism. Neither culture nor spirituality possess the ability to benefit anyone without the other. Culture needs spirituality in order to have a moral compass, and spirituality needs culture in order to be aware of its context.

The Grown-up and the Kid

IF YOU LIKE PITHY ADVICE, here is what I have. It's about the relationship between thinking and feeling, balancing emotional maturity and innocence, reconciling your outer grown-up with your inner child.

When it is time to think deeply, we each need to learn to think like an adult. We can settle our minds beyond our unevolved reactions to false threats, and beyond the false promises of instant gratification. For us grown-ups, time is short, and growing shorter by the day. We should contemplate what matters in life, and who matters, and what we would like to pass along to those people who somehow manage to arrive here next. I have written these words down—part memoir, part reflection, part humble bow to my favorite movie—because I realized that what matters most, what makes me feel the most awake and alive, is attending to my human relationships.

First, I must attend to my relationship to myself. The Buddhist teachings have offered amazing tools for moving through my resistance to my own mind a little bit more each day. Next, I should prioritize my relationship to those close to me. When it is time to think, I keep arriving at the conclusion that attending to these relationships is the most crucial thing I can do with the time remaining, however much time that might be. And finally, I contemplate my relationship to all humans, and to other beings. When I am at my most mature, I am prioritizing human relationships. When I am settled and thinking clearly, everything I do feeds this intention, each movement nourishing an act of true creativity.

And when I am *not* thinking clearly—oh boy. Then my intention gets lost, stuck within a rush-hour flood of habitually acquired triggers. When I forget my intention, dopamine and cortisol rule me, and I morph into a hungry ghost, a zombie of habit and karma.

Still, it is not always the time to think like a grown-up. Thinking clearly only gets you so far. If you *only* think, no matter how brilliant your ideas may be, you will end up anxious, doubtful, and disembodied, caught up in the Velcro entrapment of your own story line. Sometimes, it is simply time to *feel*: feel your perceptions, be who you are, and touch your humanity. And when it is time to feel, it is best to leave that grown-up behind for a little while, just like Siddhartha did under the rose apple tree, just like *The Princess Bride* invites us each to do. When it is time to feel, you might want to recall that child you once were, curious and vulnerable. Perhaps you are nine years old again, or maybe you suddenly rediscover yourself at some other point, a place where the explicit memory that visits your awareness declares a feeling of belonging, no matter the uncertainties of life. Recall the child who has not yet engrained the belief that there is some big problem with being a person. Let yourself be visited by that child frequently, the one who still leans in, opening toward the world rather than bracing or strategizing against it. Where does that memory, that tender engram, live for you?

If we are going to survive as a species, we need grown-ups to lead this world, more grown-ups than ever before. The grown-up is the one who sees clearly, eyes free from dust, reasoning beyond immediate pleasure and pain. The grown-up considers the legacy and the planet we want to leave behind with compassion for others firmly in mind.

Still, that grandchild is always here. That kid is the heart of the matter. The kid is the one who has felt each story. The kid has already received the transmission of basic goodness.

The child is the one you need to ask about true love.

APPENDIX

NOTES

ACKNOWLEDGMENTS

APPENDIX

Seven-Step Loving-Kindness
*(*Metta *or* Maitri*)*
Practice in 20–25 Minutes

(THE FOLLOWING HAS BEEN WRITTEN with great gratitude to Sharon Salzberg and Pema Chödrön for their instructions, and to William Goldman for the exemplary characters.)

BEGIN THE SESSION: Check in, and do a short mindfulness breath practice (1–5 minutes). You may also bring your hand to your heart center to activate physical awareness of your heart, rather than a conceptual experience in the brain.

TAKE THE ATTITUDE THAT YOU ARE IN A SAFE SPACE:
Imagine that your physical location is a completely safe place
to work with whatever arises in your mind. Think of the world
as a place of genuinely kind intentions (if not actions). If it is
helpful, visualize the presence of your teachers, mentors,
heroes, ancestors, or anyone who embodies unconditional
love to you, rooting you in your meditation practice, wishing
you complete success in uncovering your wisdom, compassion,
and skillful means.

PRACTICE NOTICING: For each of the seven steps that follow,
remember first to establish the presence of the person or
people you're working with. Use mindfulness to recall one
or more specific details about that person. Then scan your
reactions to the person in three areas:

   a. Discursive thoughts about them that arise;
   b. Emotions that arise; and
   c. Your physical posture when visualizing them.

PRACTICE GENERATING *METTA*: After noticing, gather the
attention to your heart center. If it is useful, imagine light
radiating out toward the person from your heart center as you
silently (or out loud, if you want) recite one or all four of the
four phrases of *metta*, slowly: "*May you (I, we) be safe, may
you be happy, may you be healthy, may you live at ease . . .*" It
can take anywhere up to 5 minutes per step. Between
consideration of each person, take three easeful breaths to
clean the slate and reestablish mindfulness in the body.

FOR AN ABBREVIATED SESSION: Do the session only for the
benefactor, yourself, and the loved one/friend. Or you could just

practice on the spot. As you move through daily life, on-the-spot loving-kindness refers to a moment when you notice yourself having a difficult moment or when another human being comes to your attention. You simply pause, hold your attention on them, and silently offer one of the four phrases noted above or a simple phrase in your own words.

Seven Steps

1. **(GRANDFATHER STAGE) IMAGINE A BENEFACTOR.** This can be a bodhisattva, a hero, or a mentor. Choose someone who inspires you easily, the closest person you can think of to a true benefactor. If you like, start by imagining this mentor or benefactor doing the practice for you. You can also imagine that a healing, silky light with warm, soothing qualities is flowing from the mentor's heart center to yours. This visualization should be used only if it helps you to feel nurtured and soothed. Eventually, you can imagine that you and your benefactor are wishing happiness to each other. Work with the benefactor for a few minutes.

    Then, *take three easeful breaths.*

    ∼

2. **(GRANDCHILD STAGE) IMAGINE YOURSELF.** Take a moment to recall your self-image before beginning to contemplate the phrases, and offer yourself loving-kindness. Practice for one or two minutes.

    Then, *take three easeful breaths.*

    ∼

3. **(FEZZIK STAGE) IMAGINE A LOVED ONE OR FRIEND.**
   This should be someone you care a lot about but with
   whom you don't always have a perfect relationship. Notice
   their presence in your mind, and offer one of or all the four
   phrases. Practice for one or two minutes.

   Then, *take three easeful breaths.*

   ~

4. **(MOVIE-EXTRA STAGE) IMAGINE A NEUTRAL PERSON.**
   This should be someone who hasn't really made much of
   an impact on you, someone you interact with regularly but
   don't really notice, a sort of "extra" on the set of your daily
   life. Examples: someone who works at a local store or a
   coworker you don't speak to. Practice for one or two
   minutes.

   Then, *take three easeful breaths.*

   ~

5. **(VIZZINI STAGE) IMAGINE AN "ENEMY."** This should
   be someone either personally known or a world
   figure who really makes it difficult for you to be
   open to or to feel anything positive for. Work with
   someone who irritates you, not someone who has
   traumatized or abused you. You could take a moment
   to imagine this person's *Princess Bride* moment, and
   imagine that they are actually experiencing happiness
   during that moment. You can also imagine the villain as
   a child and see what happens. Practice for one or two
   minutes.

   Then, *take three easeful breaths.*

   ~

6. **(WE STAGE) IMAGINE A GROUP.** Practice for a particular group of people whose suffering is touching you right now. If you are going through a hard time, you could practice for specific groups of sentient beings. For example, if you are unemployed, you could do the practice for all unemployed people, using the pronoun *we* in one or each of the four phrases. Practice for one or two minutes.

Then, *take three easeful breaths.*

~

7. **(UNIVERSAL STAGE) EXTEND OUTWARD.** Extend this intention for happiness farther and farther out from you until you are contemplating the simple phrase "May all beings be happy."

CLOSING THE SESSION: Recall a moment during the practice session of full openness and loving-kindness. Recall it both as a wordless mental state and as a physical sensation. Rest your attention in the feeling tone of this state for as long as you can before the mind wanders off. When the mind has wandered, reestablish mindfulness of the breathing body for a few final moments to close the session. Then offer yourself a bow in thanks for your right effort.

~

POSTMEDITATION EXERCISE (ON-THE-SPOT PRACTICE): Whenever you're in a group setting, notice the person your attention follows naturally and the people you tend to notice less. Shift your attention to those you naturally ignore and generate the wish "May you be happy." Odds are you ignore a lot of people, so there are no judgments in this contemplation of extras on the movie set of your daily life—just curiosity.

NOTES

Introduction

1. Nineteen eighty-seven was a great year for American movies. *The Princess Bride* was topped at the box office by many memorable films—*Fatal Attraction*, *Moonstruck*, *Dirty Dancing*, *Wall Street*, and *Spaceballs* among them, along with many movies not worth mentioning here. Number one at the box office that year: *Three Men and a Baby*, a film that precisely zero Buddhist teachers have ever contemplated in writing.

2. Bizarrely and brilliantly, *The Princess Bride* got a few mentions in the 2016 GOP presidential debates. In his article for *Time*, Patinkin said, among other things: "Every character in that movie is looking to be loved. I'm sure Ted Cruz wants to be loved. I know Donald Trump does. Everyone wants it. But we mustn't look for love by spreading hate."

3. *Trigger* has become an overused word in our language, but it is also the best translation I have found for the Tibetan word *shenpa*, which the teacher Pema Chödrön also translates as "getting hooked," the moment when an emotional reaction catches us like a trap being sprung.

4. Louis CK's bit "Everything is amazing and nobody is happy" and his discussions of loneliness could easily be early twenty-first-century Buddhist sutras.

5. Maybe the first *Matrix* movie was dharmic, I agree, but the last two really ran out of steam.

1: Mercenaries or Besties

1. The founder of the Shambhala Buddhist tradition, Chögyam Trungpa, said that the purpose of meditation is to "make friends with yourself." In my book *The Road Home: A Contemporary Exploration of the Buddhist Path* (New York: North Point Press, 2015), I refer to meditation as "accepting your own friend request."

2. David Eagleman, *The Brain: The Story of You* (New York: Pantheon, 2015).

3. Rick Hanson, *Hardwiring Happiness: The New Brain Science of Contentment, Calm, and Confidence* (New York: Harmony Books, 2013), 34.

4. The social nature of experience was even an inspiration for Shepard Fairey's wacky *Obey* art project, which began as a joke among his Rhode Island School of Design friends with the tagline "Andre the Giant Has a Posse."

5. From *The Thirty-Seven Practices of a Bodhisattva*, by the fourteenth-century monk Ngulchu Thogme, based on Ken McLeod's translation.

2: The Bad Guys

1. These three root tendencies of psychological confusion are often also referred to as "poisons."

2. Technically, Westley does not kill Vizzini. He just gives him the proverbial rope to hang himself with, or the literal iocane powder to poison himself with.

3. Mandy Patinkin, "The Real Politics in *The Princess Bride*," *Time*, December 18, 2015.

4. It is said that the historical Buddha spent a previous lifetime as a pirate who had to make very difficult decisions in the face of tyranny. In Tibetan Buddhism, many master meditators were also literal warriors of their family clans. Why couldn't a dread pirate also be a warrior of compassion?

3: Find Your Inner Fezzik

1. These scenes between Inigo and Fezzik are only in the book version, and are omitted from the movie.

2. *Road Runner* cartoons probably deserve some credit as well. To clarify, for top-notch geeks, the sand in *The Princess Bride* is actually something called "snow sand," a substance even worse to drown in than quicksand, but if you only saw the movie and didn't read the book, you'd be forgiven for assuming it was quicksand.

3. These practices, collectively known as "windhorse," are best learned in a personal setting with a teacher.

4. In our conversation about the problem with seeking revenge, Mr. Patinkin kept reiterating that revenge is a misguided attempt to fix a mistake that exists in the past. "You can't 'fix' a mistake," he insisted. "You can only move forward."

5. By all accounts, Andre the Giant had massive back problems, and even underwent surgery during and after the filming of *The Princess Bride*. He spent much of this movie, and much of his later career, hiding a back brace under his clothing. The loving giant with major back problems is a perfect metaphor to describe "burnout," or "compassion fatigue," that is, the burden of generosity in a world of seemingly endless greed.

4: There Is No Buttercup

1. The movie does not make clear where Westley must go, but in the book he heads for America, of all places, that truly mythical kingdom.

2. I would love to see a remake of *The Princess Bride* that follows the same premise of the *Ghostbusters* remake, with a total gender reversal of all key roles.

3. See the Pew poll "America's Changing Religious Landscape," Pew Research Center, May 12, 2015, http://www.pewforum.org /2015/05/12/americas-changing-religious-landscape/.

4. *Madyamaka*, or the Middle Way, was a group of Buddhist philosophical schools dedicated to explaining what emptiness meant, and how cause and effect actually functioned, both psychologically and physically.

5. I can't imagine having a romantic partner who is also your "disciple." What?!

6. In *The Road Home*, this cycle of always chasing after the next "now" is illustrated with the metaphor of a commuter. When we are lost in commute, we are always trying to get back home yet never quite arriving.

5: Lost on the High Seas

1. In the movie version of *The Princess Bride*, Westley and Buttercup are separated for five years. In the book version, they are separated for only three.

2. I have always considered zombie stories a Western thread of the classic hungry ghost tale, a narrative of the "mostly dead" places we all get caught up in, those emotional states in which we are still breathing yet too numb to be considered fully alive.

3. This student-teacher narrative, a seemingly brutal master who turns out to give the student exactly what they needed, pervades so many stories in both East and West. In the Tibetan lineage called Kagyu, this narrative appears in the story of the great Milarepa with his guru, Marpa. Milarepa is desperate to attain enlightenment because of bad karma accumulated earlier in life from harmful choices, and he holds on to this urgency

while Marpa gives him a seemingly unending list of grueling tasks that at first appear to have nothing to do with awakening. This same structure is repeated in *The Karate Kid*, *Kill Bill*, and even Christopher Nolan's reinterpretation of *Batman*: the teacher who is seemingly belligerent and selfish but who turns out to train the student to overcome their fear, doubt, and hesitation.

4. My father, David Nichtern, wrote a book called *Awakening from the Daydream: Reimagining the Buddha's Wheel of Life* (Somerville, MA: Wisdom Publications, 2016), which examines in much greater detail these classic psychological realms of Buddhism: hell, hungry ghost, animal, human, jealous god, and god.

6: Basic Goodness

1. Once again, Inigo Montoya demonstrates his wisdom in the face of uncertainty.

2. My friend Jenni Muldaur once said this when we were discussing the human tendency to date those people who aren't good for us.

3. In the book, this pivotal line is given to Fezzik's dear departed mother in a totally different context. Many masters have echoed the truth embodied in its skepticism of platitudes and salesmanship, and in the belief that life is necessarily painful.

4. It is never recommended to give your true love a dharma talk. Trust me.

5. *Virabhadra* is the Sanskrit word for "warrior." In Tibetan, it's *pawo* or *pamo*.

6. If you are waiting for a text message that may not appear, here's a trick I have learned: practice compassion meditation, and imagine everyone in your current city or town who is likewise waiting for a text message they might not ever get. It might help you feel that there is nothing wrong with your desire, and that there is also nothing wrong with its not working out for you. All of us, even Buttercup, have waited for a message that was never going to come.

7: As You Wish, Part I

1. A chapter of *The Road Home* is devoted to the practice of listening to and expressing oneself.

2. William Goldman expressed his difficulty in creating a sequel for *The Princess Bride* at the twenty-fifth-anniversary screening at the New York Film Festival in 2012. "I'm desperate to make it and write it and I don't know how," he said, according to the *Los Angeles Times.* Maybe the difficulty is based on our narrative entrenchment: we simply don't know how to tell the story of what happens after the script ends.

8: All Sentient Beings Have Been Grandpa

1. When I was a child, my father would make up spontaneous bedtime stories for me about a boy from an alien world, a kid named Boober of the planet Raltron. Boober was exactly my age, a sweet Buddhist kid with Smurf-toned skin and a Tintin-like adventurous spirit. Boober had his own private spaceship, which he used to explore foreign planets, each created on the spot from my father's imagination. For a musician, my father was top-notch at creating spontaneous narrative. If the Moth StorySLAM had existed in the 1980s and included a category for Buddhist Children's Sci-Fi, David Nichtern would surely have been crowned world champion.

2. Daniel J. Siegel, *The Developing Mind* (New York: Guilford, 2015), 51.

9: Fred Savage Is a Jerk, and I Am Fred Savage

1. Chögyam Trungpa, *Shambhala: The Sacred Path of the Warrior* (Boston: Shambhala, 2015), 9.

2. This term was coined by a friend who worked at Starbucks and had to deal with customers' constant complaints about minor imperfections in their orders.

3. In Shambhala teachings, this is also referred to as the imperial lineage.

4. In Tantric Buddhism, depending on the specific type of meditation practice you're working with, these heroic arche-

types are also called *yidams*, and also, depending on their function, "dharma protectors."

10: As You Wish, Part II

1. The classic text *The Tibetan Book of the Dead*, or the *Bardo Thodol*, goes deeply into the postdeath and prebirth experiences of consciousness. Is any of it true? Your guess is as good as mine.

Conclusion

1. Mark Epstein, for example, does a wonderful job of examining the life of Siddhartha in terms of the trauma that must have been part of his early experience, given his familial and social circumstances. When we tell people's stories, it is crucial that we treat them as human beings; otherwise we don't have anything but abstractions to look up to.

ACKNOWLEDGMENTS

FIRST, I AM NOT IN THE BUSINESS OF SHOUTING OUT people's personal lives. With the exception of my fourth-grade friend (with whom I have been trying to reconnect), everyone mentioned in this book knew I was including them in the piece, or had already written their own story publicly. I thank them all, especially my parents. I would like to honor the best friend who found me when things did get better in fifth grade, Michael Wesley Klein, who tragically passed away recently.

I need to honor my Buddhist teachers, especially Sakyong Mipham Rinpoche, Sharon Salzberg, and Suzann Duquette, for showing what it means to be part of a lineage, and still totally be yourself. Deepest thanks to everyone involved in *The Princess Bride*, especially William Goldman and Rob Reiner, for bringing so many people so many years of joy. Specifically, I got a ton out of Cary Elwes's memoir *As You Wish*, a treasure trove for geeks. I'd especially like to thank Mandy Patinkin for speaking to me about his meditation practice, the problems with revenge, and his evolving experience with this work. And deepest thanks to Christopher Guest for speaking to me and reading the manuscript, but much more important, thanks for looking after Dad all these years.

A long bow goes to my editor, Jeff Seroy, my publicist, Brian Gittis, and the Farrar, Straus and Giroux team for believing in this slightly eccentric text and shepherding it into existence. Thanks so much to Greg Pierce, Gabriella Doob, Suzanne Parker, Maud Newton, and Emily Spivack for reading early versions of this work and sharing wise feedback. And to Lisa Weinert, who is not only my amazing agent but one of my oldest friends. Thanks for letting me be weird, and precisely discerning the relevance of my weirdness to a public audience.

Thank you to all the wise dharma students I have interacted with over the past fifteen to sixteen years. Your thousands of insights on relationships are the primary source for my thoughts on the matter. To all my personal

Fezziks and Inigos of all genders, not a moment goes by that I don't feel grateful for your friendship. Just a few who went way above and beyond the call of duty during the writing of this book were Juan Carlos Castro, Jeff Zimbalist, Greg Pierce, and Jamie Isaia.

And finally to my wife, Marissa Dutton, thank you. I marvel at your ability to do all the things you do. And now that you've also done them while simultaneously creating a person, I think you might just be showing off.